TREASURES
OF
DARKNESS

TREASURES

OF

DARKNESS

COBY MCGEE

ARPress
ILLUMINATING IDEAS.
EMPOWERING VOICES

ARPress
45 Dan Road Suite 5
Canton MA 02021
Hotline: 1(888) 821-0229
Fax: 1(508) 545-7580

Ordering Information:

Quantity sales. Special discounts are available on quantity purchases by corporations, associations, and others. For details, contact the publisher at the address above.

Printed in the United States of America.

ISBN-13:   Softcover   979-8-89330-364-3
              eBook   979-8-89330-365-0
Library of Congress Control Number: 2024900787

TREASURES OF DARKNESS

by Coby L. McGee

Reviewed by: Barbara Bamberger Scott

Author McGee combines lively memoir and Christian mysticism in this look at life and its possibilities. As a young child, the author didn't realize what an abusive father he'd had, but he does have memories of the step fathers who followed and their more subtle forms of disdain. He notes that at all ages, one can have fears; and though one may out grow some of them, fears are part of the human psyche that, as he learned, can be relieved by one's closeness to God. Part of that process entails the willingness to forgive even the worst of one's enemies, like remodeling a house, in which advice will be needed and major changes affected.

A destructive storm and a godly supervisor at McGee's college job taught him that "almost anything can be repaired or replaced." Following a failed marriage and the love he sustained for his three children, McGee began his healing journey, overcoming highly negative, self-abnegating thoughts and even a wish to end his life. He was urged by a Christian mentor to totally forgive those who had done him wrong. It became for him a "rainbow experience" that he wishes to share with others.

McGee, a Texas businessman, has a true talent for weaving words, mining often traumatic examples from his experience to produce straightforward, spiritually based advice to readers. As told from a Christian standpoint, his childhood was one of abuse and confusion, his adulthood one of achievement mixed with emotional chaos and often extremely grim, self-destructive imagery. Yet the narrative clearly shows that these times of darkness, mingled with his personal determination and vibrant faith, have brought him to a place of peace. His autobiographical, philosophical viewpoint work can provide an engaging focus for group discussion and individual contemplation for those seeking to understand themselves more deeply and improve relationships with others.

TABLE OF CONTENTS

CHAPTER 1

WELCOME TO PLANET EARTH

What walks on four legs in the morning, two legs at noon, and three legs in the evening?" This is a famous riddle from Greek mythology that was posed to Oedipus by the great Sphinx. In order for Oedipus to pass through to the city of Thebes he had to answer this riddle correctly, or be eaten by the hideous Sphinx monster. Luckily for him, he answered correctly, "Man."

This is a clever metaphor about the human condition. First, we learn to crawl on all fours as a baby, then we eventually learn to walk on two legs, then in our twilight years require the assistance of a cane (third leg) to get around. Our lives here on earth are pretty short if you really think about it. I just turned 60 and it seems like just the other day I was 25, full of energy and excited about the future.

I absolutely loved being a daddy to my 3 kids, but they grew up so fast. I miss those days of their youth, watching cartoons with them, playing and wrestling on the floor with them. But now they are all adults, my boys Jacob and Aaron already graduated from college and my only daughter Macy is just starting. Life has flown by in some ways. I've seen great success and devastating losses in my life, but the Lord has been faithful to see me through it all.

The Bible states that God "has set eternity in every man's heart" (Ecclesiastes 3:11), meaning that we all have a desire to know where we came from, where we are going, and what our purpose on this planet is. We humans tend to "fail forward," meaning we usually make all the wrong choices first before we realize there are better choices out there. Hopefully, we make better decisions as we get older.

Life is filled with suffering, even when we make decent choices, but there are things we do to ourselves that create unnecessary suffering. I've learned a lot of things the hard way, and I learned the greatest lessons during the darkest times of my life.

Hopefully this book will help alleviate some of your unnecessary suffering and give you hope in the dark times of your life. If you've been asking, "Where is God?" when things are falling apart, then you've picked up the right book.

Did you know that you have been created in God's image? That's what the Bible says. Of all the creatures that exist or have ever existed on the earth, which one is the most impressive? Lions, tigers, elephants? What about dinosaurs? Of all God's creations, humans have the most highly developed cognitive aptitude, physical dexterity and the ability to change their environment. Even now, artificial intelligence is attempting to create what would be a perfect human, but we have something AI can never have…a human spirit.

I'm sure you've heard of near death experiences, or actual death experiences, where people confess their spirit came out of the body for a time. Our human spirit is the eternal part of us, and it is the aspect of humans that allows us to connect with God. The Bible states that God is a Spirit, and those that worship Him do so in spirit and in truth.

With our mind we learn about God's attributes, but with our spirit we experience Him personally.

If we think about our physical body, especially when we are a newborn baby, we find ourselves in a very vulnerable, very needy state. I know we've seen footage of farm animals being born and they stand up and walk almost immediately. Well, God in all of His wisdom designed us to be very dependent on our mothers and fathers for food, shelter, clothing, protection, and even to wipe our tiny little hineys for the first couple of years of our lives.

I remember thinking as a soon-to-be father that changing a diaper was going to be the worst part of being a parent. As it turned out, changing my kids' diapers was one of the easiest parts of parenthood. Lol! Parents of teenagers know what I'm talking about. I've wondered at times, "Why did God make humans so weak and needy as babies, when some animals are able to start walking around right after they're born?"

That is one of the many things that makes humans different from other creatures. We've been made to undergo a process of bonding with other humans; most importantly with our parents.

Babies need to be held by mom or dad when they are fed for several months, whether nursed or bottle fed. This is comforting for the baby and very fulfilling as a parent. I remember when Jacob, our firstborn, was little. After supper I would be sitting in the living room in my easy chair. When my wife would finish nursing Jacob, she would bring him to me, lay him on my chest, and we would both nod off for a while.

That was a safe, comfortable place for Jacob to rest after a good meal, but it was also one of the most special and fulfilling experiences of my life as a new Daddy. It was good for both of us. God designed us to start off our lives in a safe, warm environment, protected and provided for by people who love us. This is God's perfect plan, but as we all know, things don't always go according to plan.

I was fortunate enough to have a sweet, loving mom when I was little. She was attentive and affectionate, and I honestly loved the attention I got from her whenever I got sick. It was really nice feeling loved and cared for, and it made being sick not such a bad experience. I thank God for giving me a good mom, but I questioned God's choice of dads for many years.

I'm not going to bash my Dad, or either of my two step-dads in this book; I could just as easily have had a great dad and a bad mom for that matter. It doesn't matter in the long run. The fact is, this is an imperfect world with imperfect people, and most people treat others the same way their parents treated them, even if that behavior was abusive or neglectful.

Unhealthy patterns of behavior and beliefs can be repeated from generation to generation without anyone realizing it is abusive. There were patterns of abuse and mental illness set into my family of origin long before I was born, which affected me long into my adult life.

The good news is, we are not alone in our struggles. There are other humans we can learn from who have overcome great obstacles, and we also have access to a loving, powerful, all-knowing God that is eager to help us along the way.

Another vulnerability that we deal with as humans is our souls' need for love, belonging and connection to others. Our sense of well-being is greatly affected by our need for physical touch, words of affirmation and proximity to others. As a child learns to walk and talk, he begins to explore his environment and develop skills. Then the child goes to daycare, church and school for socialization and the development of his soul (mind, will and emotions).

I personally had some hurtful experiences in daycares as a preschooler, but had some great experiences in grade school. I guess that's just the luck of the draw, so to speak. Hopefully we had good experiences with mom and dad as children, but when we get out into the world, we find out that some people are safe and some are not.

My mom had to leave my alcoholic, abusive dad when I was 4, my older sister 5, and my baby sister just a newborn. We left our home in Midland and moved to Lubbock, Texas in 1966 in order to escape an abusive environment and start a new life. As a little boy that had just left his home, his town and his friends it was very challenging on an emotional level.

I was too young to remember the abuse that we suffered at the hands and words of our Daddy, but my big sister and my Mom told me about it when I got older. However, even though my mind couldn't remember those experiences, my subconscious mind had certainly taken some notes.

Just being present in an unsafe environment as a toddler affected my sense of safety. As we began to settle into our new home in Lubbock, I occasionally suffered feelings of fear and abandonment. Since my mom was now a single parent, she had to go to work and I had to go to daycare.

In order to help my mom, my grandparents kept my big sister with them in Rule, Texas to go to kindergarten. Rhonda was a year older than me so we were playmates and best friends, but now she wasn't there either. It was an emotionally upsetting time for me since so much had changed overnight.

We as children are very innocent, vulnerable and tender to every stimulus that we encounter. We can't filter out negative experiences, so we are affected by everything. Only as adults can we go back and resolve the negative effects of our youth. Sometimes our current suffering is a result of unresolved or unprocessed pain from the past even as far back as birth. It's not our fault that we take on trauma as children.

I just want to say that overcoming emotional pain is as simple in theory as overcoming physical wounds. Physical wounds heal by certain methods, and so do emotional wounds; it's just that for some cruel reason humans shame each other for having emotional and mental struggles. This is a great evil that we pass on to our own kind.

I want to help bring a change of consciousness to the whole arena of mental and emotional illness so that we can learn how to heal from the trauma we experience. It has taken me a lifetime to allow God to speak to the broken places in my heart. I now want to share these truths and perspectives with you so you don't have to suffer as long as I did. May God bless you as you continue to read further.

CHAPTER 2

INNOCENCE LOST

I wonder how God felt when Adam and Eve couldn't manage to obey the one command he gave them in the garden of Eden? I'm thinking of those hilarious memes on YouTube of "You had just one job." Think about it…God places you in the garden of Eden, a perfect environment where you walked and talked with the Lord every evening and you lacked no good thing.

The only thing you were told to stay away from was the tree of the knowledge of good and evil. "If you eat its fruit you will surely die." He was not talking about immediate physical death, but a death of our innocence, peace of mind and the feeling of connection with our Creator.

God's commands are for our protection, not to withhold blessing from us. Also, there is no reason to steal from God or manipulate him for your needs; He says, "Just ask, and you will receive." All created beings start out with a sense of scarcity of supply. It's basically a fear of the unknown. That's shown by a baby's desperate cries for food when they're hungry. It's as if they fear there will be no more food.

One of God's greatest blessings to us is to give us a free will, but we are not smart or strong or noble enough to always choose what is best for us. Eve was easily swayed to eat the fruit from the one tree that was off limits, and Adam was easily swayed to follow along. Of course what man is going to say no to a beautiful naked woman standing in front of him? Lol! But seriously, how easy was it for the serpent to deceive the humans and disobey God's warning?

I've been deluded along with many others into thinking that we would have never eaten that apple. Yeah, right! We would have done the exact same thing, and you know why? Because we as humans are gullible, selfish, arrogant, foolish and envious people by nature, and we all make stupid choices. It's usually not until we suffer the consequences of our bad choices that we seek out better ones.

Why do we think we're better than others? The Bible calls us out on this when it says, "Why do you complain about the speck of dust in your brother's eye when you have a plank in your own eye?" I believe it all goes back to the original sin committed in the garden of Eden.

Most people think the original sin was disobedience by eating the "apple" but the sin that occurred before that was actually the sin of envy. The serpent told Eve that God just didn't want them to know what He knows, that He was withholding information from them. The serpent was tempting Eve with jealousy and envy.

Let's go even further back, to when it was just God, Jesus, the Holy Spirit and the angels in heaven. Lucifer was one of the three Archangels, along with Gabriel and Michael. Now Lucifer was the most beautiful of all the angels, the Bible describing him as having multiple musical instruments connected to him in some manner.

So Lucifer was given special beauty and abilities, but he was still created to worship and serve the Most High God. Lucifer became proud in his heart because of his special beauty and talents, and began to want special attention.

I guess God gave even the angels free will to obey him or not, because Lucifer became envious of God's power and authority over all things, and decided to rebel against the Lord. He managed to take a third of the angels with him in rebellion, and so God cast them all out of heaven.

God changed Lucifer's name to Satan after that because he no longer identified as an angel of "light" in the eyes of the Lord. Satan was envious of God's power, authority and of the worship God received in heaven. He lacked no good thing, but he just wanted more. So that begs the question, why didn't God just create perfectly obedient beings to share His life and love with?

To answer that question we must discuss the nature of love as God sees it. The word of God says that true love is kind, patient, unselfish, not demanding, not pushy and several other things. God wants to be loved just as we want to be loved, not out of obligation or manipulation, but out of someone's own free will.

Obviously, Satan wasn't satisfied with a perfect heaven, and Adam and Eve were not satisfied with a perfect Eden, so God understands the nature of created beings. Created beings tend to not be content with what's been given to them, and contentment and gratitude are only learned through experiencing loss.

I see widespread discontent in these current generations. I grew up in the 60's and 70's where we were made to do chores, to babysit, to work paper routes and mow lawns for our money. It taught us the value of money and the appreciation of earning what we bought. My kids, born at the turn of the 21st century were given every luxury just because our lifestyles and culture demanded it.

I remember my daughter Macy begging me to buy her an I-phone when she was 10 years old because supposedly, "EVERYBODY else has one." I held her off for 2 years, enduring the consistent begging and pleading that she was so good at. So, when she turned 12, I gave in because apparently school required her to have one. All 3 of my kids had an I-phone long before I had one. I didn't see what the big deal was. A phone's a phone right? I had no idea…

I regret that decision to this day. I'm going to make some of you angry by saying this, but giving so many electronic gadgets to young children gives them a false sense of reality, and basically distracts them from real life and real relationships. We should let our kids stare out the car window on road trips instead of putting some device in their hands.

LET them be bored! It's good for the soul, and they need time to just sit and think about whatever pops into their mind. Our kids have lost the ability to sit alone and ponder life. They are constantly distracted by electronic devices. And the ability to Google information in an instant can be nice at times but it has made parents obsolete. It can ruin God's original plan for children to learn about life from their parents. That just needed to be said.

So my generation grew up learning to earn their keep, make friends by playing outdoors, get lots of sun and exercise, and basically learned hands-on ways of existing in the world. Our kids stay inside and play video games. And don't even get me started on all of the deception, temptation and personal agendas we are all exposed to through our computers and phones.

Basically, what I'm trying to say is that our current society is spoiled with luxuries that most humans throughout history were never afforded, and instead of being content, we just demand more. We aren't satisfied with an I-phone 40 (exaggeration for effect), we must have the newest version of everything.

Think about this…our great grandparents probably lived on farms, grew their own food and rode around on horses, or walked. What a nightmare to have to walk to school or the store! Our kids have no clue how easy they have it compared to 95% of the people that lived before us. Of course they have been exposed to more temptations than we ever were.

We don't even have to go to a movie theater anymore; we just order a movie from Netflix or some other streaming app. Standing outside a movie theater in the 70's on a Friday night used to be the event of the week, and it came with the added anticipation of possibly finding a boyfriend or girlfriend. Nowadays, you have to go online to meet someone. Kids may prefer that, but it is just completely awkward for older adults. Don't get me started on that subject.

We humans were designed by God to grow intellectually, socially, emotionally and spiritually and we were meant to learn by working and failing and getting up and fighting again. We need challenges, we even need bullies at times, to bring out the best in us. We become strong by lifting heavy weights, and we grow in character by facing and working through challenges. Our confidence grows as we face our fears and stand up to challenges.

Being given too much without earning it has led many of us to lack appreciation for what we have, and to feel entitled to everything our neighbor has. If you feel envious of what your neighbor has, then do the same work they did and earn what they've earned. When you know you've struggled to earn something, you appreciate it much more than if it was given to you.

Another lesson from the garden of Eden story includes the realization that God made man out of the dust, out of the basic elements from the periodic table we studied in chemistry class. But it was the very breath of God that gave life to the body of Adam.

God's very name in Hebrew is YHWH, or Yahweh, which can easily be thought of as the sounds we make as we inhale and exhale. While getting a minor degree in Biology in college I saw the incredible complexity of the human body, but none of it would work without God's very breath in our lungs. He is the very air that we breathe and the source of life for our bodies, our minds, our emotions, and our spirits.

Colossians 1:17 says that, "... in (Jesus) all things hold together." That has become one of my favorite passages of scripture in recent years, knowing Jesus held me together at times when I thought I would fall apart.

Another lesson from the garden was that God made Adam and Eve perfect and innocent. They were both naked, but felt no shame. They didn't know the difference between good and evil because they were innocent. They were as innocent as little children, and their lives were pretty sweet. They got to walk and talk with God in the evenings face to face and heart to heart. That will be restored when we get to heaven by the way. It's what God intended in the first place for us humans. But the moment Eve and Adam ate the fruit of the tree of the knowledge of good and evil that all changed.

While in Bible College in Dallas, I read a book about the story of Adam and Eve, and it described the emotions that they felt after disobeying God's warning about that tree. As I read about the feelings of shame, embarrassment and loss of innocence they felt after eating the apple I literally broke down in tears. I could just imagine what it was like to have perfect fellowship with God the Father, and suddenly feel the separation, isolation and loneliness they must have experienced. The shame they felt made them feel the need to hide from God.

At times in my life I have felt those feelings of separation, loneliness, shame and loss of innocence because of my experiences as a child. I know what it's like to suffer emotionally for years over trauma that was not my fault. It just broke my heart for Adam and Eve, and for the rest of mankind, to know we've lost the perfect relationship with our true Father God because of our sin.

It was heartbreaking for me to witness my children's loss of innocence as they grew up. Hearing how Jacob's best friend thoughtlessly betrayed him in front of the whole class, seeing Aaron's personality change overnight because a daycare worker shamed him harshly merely for spilling some milk, and watching Macy's innocence be robbed from her through that I-phone she desperately wanted, and her experiences with mean girls.

Sin separates us from God. But God has made a way for our sin to be washed away, forgiven and the penalty of sin to be paid…by the blood of an innocent human being, His son Jesus. I've wondered at times how hard it must have been for Jesus to leave his place at the right hand of the Father's throne in heaven, and come down to earth and have a human experience.

He had perfect communion with his Father God, and all the angels of heaven worshiping him all day long, and surrounded with glory and honor. But because Adam and Eve sinned, and mankind came under the curse of sin from that moment on, there had to be a way to redeem mankind back to relationship with God.

The Hebrew people understand the concept of animal sacrifices very well. For generations, the Hebrews were allowed by God to sacrifice an innocent lamb at certain times to pay for their sins. This was a temporary fix for an ongoing problem, separation from God.

At the appointed time, God sent Jesus to the earth to experience the human condition, while still holding all of his attributes as the Son of God. He lived 33 years on earth as a man (Son of Man) while also being the very image of God (Son of God) as described in Colossians 1:15.

Until we are reconnected to our relationship with God through trust in Jesus, we still operate under the curse of shame, loss of innocence and loneliness. We are lost because we are separated in our spirit and soul from the presence of God. When we confess our faith in God, through acceptance of Jesus as Lord and Savior, our human spirit is made alive by the Spirit of God. This is referred to as being "born of the Spirit of God."

He actually comes to dwell in our body. We become a temple (dwelling place) of the Holy Spirit. At this point we can have fellowship with God, who is a Spirit. There is a whole other realm of existence that we have access to that affects our bodies, souls and spirit. And the Spirit realm rules over the natural realm. We shall discuss that later also.

To summarize what we've learned from the garden of Eden...

1) Humans are naturally envious of others and want power and control over others.

2) We aren't very bright. We are easily manipulated and tempted.

3) We tend to not appreciate what is given to us; we always want more.

4) We don't like to be told what to do.

5) We don't make good choices until we've made all the bad ones first.

6) Without connection to our heavenly Father we feel lost and shameful.

7) God's plan has always been to have intimate relationship with humans.

CHAPTER 3

SHAME ON US

As I've studied and researched human nature, basically to determine if I was normal or not, I found two primal mindsets of men and women. Women, as they have admitted, suffer from a baseline feeling of fear. They are scared of animals, insects, men, the weather, you name it. They crave safety and comfort and they seek out a man to provide safety to them.

Men are troubled with the fear of not being good enough for our women and families. We crave the affections of a beautiful woman, and we feel our best whenever we are providing, protecting and serving them. We know women want a good provider, so we will wear ourselves out to please and provide for our women and children. We feel lost without a purpose and someone to serve. These are the common baseline feelings of humans, but what lies beneath both of those is the subconscious sense of shame.

Remember, Adam and Eve were naked and felt no shame, until they were given the knowledge of good and evil. We feel shame because we are aware of our human frailties and ignorance. We know we are stupid at times, and selfish, and jealous and everything else. When we get hurt, we cry sometimes, and we hate that people see us cry. We want desperately to feel powerful, strong and in control, but deep down we know we are weak and fearful of many things.

When I was probably 5 years old I was playing outside with my cousins in their neighborhood. The football was thrown over my head, and as I was retrieving it from under an old abandoned truck, something scared me. The bumper on that truck was shaped and painted like it had fangs, so to me it looked like a monster that wanted to eat me!

As children, silly things scare us that adults don't even think about, but as we grow older, the things we fear grow along with us. Babies are scared of loud noises, kids are scared of monsters and scary looking trucks, teenagers are scared of not fitting in, and adults are scared of not having enough money, and of being alone.

These are all common, age-appropriate fears that we outgrow as we get older, generally speaking. But there are fears that are innate to us as humans, that are a part of our fallen human nature that haunt us until we discover the truth about ourselves, and our world, and about God.

There is the shame of being naive, ignorant, physically weak, powerless over certain things— the list is endless. One of the blessings of growing old is that, as we face our fears, silly or real, and overcome them, we grow in confidence. This type of shame is not necessarily bad, because it motivates us to become wise, educated, go to the gym, eat right and learn the skills that we want to acquire. Knowledge is power, and the pursuit of knowledge and understanding is one of the greatest joys we can experience.

I love learning new things, acquiring new skills. I've done a lot of home remodeling in my spare time through the years, and I've picked up a lot of advice from skilled tradesmen and women. That knowledge has made me a lot of money through remodeling and real estate investment. I learned the value of asking for help.

There is no shame in being ignorant, only in staying ignorant. We are constantly faced with new challenges and circumstances that are unfamiliar to us, so we are always in a state of seeking truth and wisdom. I encourage you to find the courage to try new things, learn new skills; it's what makes life fun and rewarding.

A basic pattern of shame has been passed down from generation to generation because of our ignorance, lack of patience and lack of understanding. For example, consider a mother who has taken her children with her to the grocery store. If that child is 6 or under he has a very short attention span, and is easily influenced by what he sees.

And try to avoid the toy aisle at all costs! Just take my word for it; you will regret it! Kids are just bound to get upset about something in the grocery store, whether they want something they can't have, get scolded for running off, or just by being bored or tired.

So, 9 times out of 10 that parent will scold or shame their child into behaving because shaming is the quickest way to change behavior, even if it is a hurtful method. There are better kinder ways to remedy the behavior, and if this happened in the privacy of home, the parent could address the situation with more patience and compassion. Children's hearts are much more tender than adults, so those harsh words do more damage than we realize.

I was talking to a man the other day about being disciplined as a child. His mom was scolding and shaming him for doing something, and he was wishing at the time she would just spank him instead of talking that way. I bet we've all felt that way. Discipline should involve instruction, but does not have to include shaming our kids.

Remember, we need to be taught everything about life. We are not like animals who have more basic instincts on how to operate and survive. We are much more needy of being taught how to live. Our lives are much more complicated than wild animals and we are at the mercy of our parents and grandparents in setting us up and pointing us in the right direction.

There are many important life lessons that we are never taught in school, college or church, so it is up to us to seek out understanding for ourselves. We can't blame others for our ignorance, which keeps us in a victim mentality. It's up to us to dig deeper for the answers. I love this passage of scripture in Proverbs 26:2,

"It is the glory of God to conceal a matter, and to search out a matter is the glory of kings."

And this one from Romans 12:2,

"Do not conform any longer to the pattern of this world, but be transformed by the renewing of your mind."

If we refuse to repeat the basic patterns of life and search for higher truth, we become like kings on earth, and discover the true riches of life. Ask for advice from those wiser than you. Blaze your own trail by following your own conscience. We don't have to just repeat what everybody else has done. God created you to be different from everybody else. Unfortunately, most of us just want to blend in and fit in with the crowd.

Another story of how shame affected a friend of mine was at church summer camp when I was in high school. One day, we were told to get into groups and devise a skit that would tell a moral or lesson for everyone, and the best skit would win a prize on the last day of camp.

Some of the older guys, including me, decided to do a really silly skit where we oiled our bodies up and had our version of a Mr. America contest. So on Friday, when it was our turn, we got up on stage, declared ourselves to be the "Spiritual Giants" and just started flexing our muscles. It was meant to be funny, of course.

The girls were laughing their heads off at our silly skit, which is what we expected, and we actually won the prize for best skit! But when we were up there I glanced around and saw the only freshman that was in our skit. He was younger and naturally smaller than us seniors, so he was straining really hard to look as muscular as the rest of us. His face was so red from the strain it was cracking me up.

I know this freshman was embarrassed that he didn't look as big or strong as the rest of us, but it didn't dawn on me until many years later how that experience affected him. We lost contact for many years after high school, but we became Facebook friends as adults. Most of his posts were about his workouts and weightlifting competitions. The shame he felt that day had a big effect on him. Many professional athletes are driven to succeed because of not measuring up as a younger person.

There is also a more cruel and intrusive type of shame that can alter our personality for years, until we are made aware of it. There is a demonic spirit of shame that can take a strong hold of our thoughts and emotions through either a traumatic experience, or prolonged exposure to abuse. This type of shame can't be overcome just by learning new life skills. My soul was subjected to this type of shame when I was a 3-year-old child.

My older sister told me this story decades later when we were talking about our experiences with our 3 dads. She told the story of my birth father taking me and her to the park to play one day. Apparently I had taken a fall while playing and had skinned up my knee and started to cry. Remember, I was just three years old.

Maybe I should preface this story with an insight into my dad first. My mom said he was a pretty good husband until the day he became a father, at which time he began to go to the bars in the evenings instead of coming home to his wife and kids. Something snapped in him that either scared him or overwhelmed him about being a father. Apparently this is not uncommon. Many years ago one of our friends from church put a shotgun in his mouth the week before his first child was born. He was the leader of our young married couples' group. It shocked everyone!

I'm not judging anyone here, because I was a father of young kids too. I know that women are much better suited to deal with small children. It can be tough for a man to handle a crying baby. The high pitch of their screams alone is painful to a man's eardrums. I'm not making excuses, just an observation. Back to my story…

So there we were at the park. I had just hurt myself and was crying about it, and it would have been great if I had been picked up, dusted off and comforted by my daddy, but that's not what happened. I can only assume my dad was embarrassed by my crying and the negative attention it brought to our situation. It is also very likely that he had been drinking. His embarrassment and frustration led him to shame me and kick me as I lay on the ground crying. A 3-year-old!

It really doesn't matter how hard he kicked me or exactly what words he used to shame me; just the mere experience for my tender 3-year-old heart was enough to leave a scar in my subconscious mind for the next 50 years of my life. And there's no telling how many other abusive experiences were registered in my subconscious mind during those days. Our mom told us some scary stories of his drunken rages.

But like I said earlier, I didn't consciously remember those experiences at all; my sister told me this as an adult. Only in a counseling session as a 57-year-old man did the Holy Spirit reveal this to me. There is a beautiful ending to this story which I'll reveal in a later chapter, but for now this just explains the way shame entered my life at such a young age, having a profound effect on nearly every single relationship of my life.

It especially affected my relationship with myself as I grew older, making me feel like I had to suppress my need to be comforted. I didn't allow myself to express negative feelings, because I might get punished for it. As I grew older, I suppressed my needs, and sought only to meet the needs of others. This is a very common response to living with an abusive, alcoholic parent, and it's called codependency.

That is certainly a more extreme example of how shame enters our lives, but it's more common than we may think. Most parents don't even realize what they are doing is abusive, because that's how they were treated as children as well. This is just a cruel pattern passed down through the generations, and it's so common we don't even give it a second thought.

My birth father was not a good influence on me. He was an alcoholic, a narcissist and was just plain mean when he was drunk. The only "advice" I remember receiving from him was telling me how to manipulate women in order to get laid. I believe I was 15 years old at the time. Yeah, great influence.

I've admonished my adult children to be aware of the increasing deception in the world and even in our churches, and to seek out the truth in all things that concern them. If you don't feel right about something, listen to your inner voice and seek out more information on the subject. The Bible is the greatest source of truth that exists, and it includes very practical, everyday wisdom on how to live. 1 Peter 1:18 says God can redeem us from the empty way of life that's been handed down to us from our ancestors. That's the good news.

Let me finish this subject on the power of shame by just saying this. I've talked about our human frailty, our unhealthy tendencies, our basic ignorance about all things, and our need to learn and seek truth in all things. Unfortunately, it takes effort and courage to face our weaknesses and our fears, so many of us revert to blaming others for our bad behavior so we don't have to face our own junk.

I want to take a moment to refer you to a lady named Brene' Brown. I was introduced to her work a few years ago and was very impressed. She has spent a great deal of time researching, interviewing and counseling people regarding the influences of shame.

She is an excellent resource if you want to really dive deep into the subject. I have great respect and appreciation for her and her desire to help people heal. She has great books and great YouTube videos. I'm just able to give a layman's insight into these subjects, and what I've learned has been out of necessity and by the grace of God.

CHAPTER 4

OUR RESPONSE TO PAIN

I know God gives us all different personality types, with different strengths and weaknesses. I like the fact that God states in Psalm 139 that it was He who formed us in the womb and by his wisdom created our inmost parts. He has a reason and a plan for everyone that is born, and he has already equipped us from birth with the aptitudes and personalities to accomplish our assignment.

I used to despise the fact that I had a melancholy personality, and was so sensitive to certain things. When I was a small child, even though I had experienced life-affecting trauma in my subconscious, I still had a pretty normal childhood. My older sister Rhonda and I played together a lot and she taught me a lot of stuff, even how to get into trouble.

My mom told me that when we were little, Rhonda would do my talking for me, lol. I guess she liked having a little brother to control and boss around. Mom eventually told her to let me speak for myself, thank goodness. But I actually didn't mind taking a back seat, following others' lead, and just tagging along. My cousins were all a few years older than me, so I often followed them around and did what they wanted to do.

My laid back, passive role as younger brother, younger cousin was comfortable for me for many years, but I eventually had to stand on my own two feet when I got into grade school. In first grade one day I had to pee really bad. Our teacher always said if anyone needed to go, to raise their hand. Every time I raised my hand someone else would beat me to it, so my eyeballs were floating by the time I finally got my turn, lol.

As I closed the door behind me, I just couldn't hold it in any longer and just peed all over myself! I started crying, and the whole class knew it. That was just me being the last one to fight for my needs. That's a funny example of my shyness, but there were so many times that I would not stand up for my rights or needs. Whatever the reason, most of my life I felt that other people had a right to get their needs met before mine.

My mom divorced my dad when I was 4 years old, but he would occasionally come to see us kids whenever the mood struck him. The night of my graduation ceremony, he took me to dinner, and in between his flirtations with the waitress, commissioned me for a job that was never mine to have. He said, "Since I'm not around anymore, you need to take care of your sisters for me." I immediately thought, "But that's your job."

That is one of the classic ways narcissistic, alcoholic people pass off their responsibilities to others. I've seen households where the child is more mature than the adult. That is emotional and mental abuse of a child. Even though I knew it was messed up, there's a fine line between helping people and rescuing people from their own responsibilities. People need to take responsibility for their own lives, and when we rescue them, it prevents them from growing.

The relationship between the narcissist and codependent is well studied because it is so common, in fact, narcissism is quickly becoming the worst epidemic of the 21st century. The rise of technology, the credit system of attaining goods, and the extravagant luxuries that we enjoy on a daily basis has ruined our relationships. We've become spoiled, entitled, impatient and selfish like no other time in history.

Our children don't need their parents anymore because Siri and Google have taken their place. YouTube and TikTok now teach our children what is popular, causing our basic morals and human kindness to erode away. Facebook has emboldened us to ridicule and shame people from a distance, and therefore we don't suffer the consequences of our bad behavior.

When I was a kid we all went outside and played sports after school, interacting with each other and learning how to get along with each other. Now, social media allows kids to say whatever they want without repercussions. There is no social accountability anymore, therefore our kids are rarely called out or corrected. They assume their opinion is right as long as a few people "like" their posts.

These things have fostered the rise of self-absorbed, "look at me" mindsets that have changed the whole atmosphere of public schools, universities, and even our churches. This is pure narcissism! It is a me-first attitude that only cares about self. It is ego driven and manipulative and is destroying the giving nature of sweet people.

These narcissists seek out kind people to meet their needs because they know they will put up with abuse for years and years. I certainly put up with the narcissists in my life for years, until I got sick of it and confronted it.

After listening to a friend's stories about the abuses her family heaped on her, I see that she was not allowed to have her voice as a child. She was not allowed to object to her parents' wishes even when they were abusive. Boundaries were consistently broken down by the adults in her life, so that she had to build a wall of defensiveness around her heart just to survive. She finds it very difficult to trust people and to believe that anyone has truly good intentions towards her.

She had to cut off her emotional self and put on a fake "happy mask" in order to avoid being shamed by her family for being a normal child with normal emotions. She acted happy on the outside, but was consumed with rage and shame and envy on the inside. My experience doesn't seem as bad in comparison.

I longed to have a girlfriend during my adolescent and young adult years, but I was somewhat shy, even though I was attractive to the ladies. I was just stunted emotionally because of my lack of proper attachment to my Daddy as a child. Psychologists will tell you it's the father relationship that gives the child the proper feeling of confidence. Sorry, ladies that's just how God designed it. But the child learns emotional and social bonding from the mother.

When your emotions get wounded deeply as a child, you literally stop growing emotionally until the blockage is removed, until the hurt is healed. Narcissists can almost never accept responsibility for their failures, they must deny or blame others for their behavior. There is no way to heal from trauma if you never take responsibility to seek healing, when you just stay in a constant state of victimhood, blaming other people for your pain.

Humans tend to respond to conflict with defensiveness at first. Our pride, our shame, our feelings of fear and rejection all kick in, making it very difficult to resolve any conflict. It takes two open-minded, humble people to resolve conflicts. We have to leave our insecurities behind, and focus on the shared goal of unity and cooperation in order to find a healthy solution.

If a couple can't feel safe enough to talk things out without getting defensive, they can never resolve any conflict. Research says couples actually grow stronger bonds as they resolve conflicts together. Our basic human fears can prevent the process of growth by making us shy away from processing our feelings with one another.

We were created to bond with other humans, to need their support and to give us alternate perspectives about us. We all have blindspots, just like we do while driving a car. We have strengths and weaknesses, and we are generally drawn to people who are strong where we are weak, and vice versa. We need each other. That's why God says it's not good for man to be alone.

Our shame wants us to isolate ourselves from others. We don't want to ask for help for fear of being ridiculed, even when we need help the most. That is the worst thing about human nature; we hide from people when we need them the most.

So what do many people do when they feel hurt, rejected and lonely, but don't feel safe enough to ask for help? All manner of coping devices, from overeating, to drugs, promiscuity, binging on Netflix, drinking-- basically anything and everything to distract us from feeling our feelings.

When I was young and I was upset about something, I would get my basketball and shoot baskets for long periods of time. I continued that practice for the rest of my life. When I was upset I'd go shoot hoops; that's why I have such a sweet stroke even at my age. Lol. Exercise is actually a great way to calm down when we are upset. Since I have a degree in Exercise and Sport Science, I know exercise is one of the best ways to rid our bodies of stress.

Emotional stress stimulates our "Fight or Flight" adrenaline response, and exercise burns off the excess adrenaline. After our body recovers from the excess adrenaline, we can calm down enough to think rationally about the stressor. My favorite mode of calming down from an acute stress response is either running, basketball, or most satisfying– hitting some baseballs. I would pretend the baseball was my problem and knock the crap out of it. Very satisfying; and a healthier way to calm down.

But the most common response to the pain we feel in life is to seek distraction from that pain. If we allowed ourselves to talk about our sufferings without the fear of rejection, maybe we wouldn't have to suffer so much and for so long. Another cruel irony is that when people hurt us, we find it hard to open up to other humans for fear of more rejection. When I couldn't find the help I needed in a church setting, I found compassion in various support groups from people who have experienced losses.

What if there was a person who was just so loving, nurturing and compassionate that we could say anything at all to? Wouldn't that be nice? Did you realize Jesus suffered every pain that we experience when He lived on the earth for 33 years?

"For we do not have a high priest who is unable to sympathize with our weaknesses, but we have one who has been tempted in every way, just as we are..." Hebrews 4:15

I'm so blessed to have found a relationship with Jesus at a young age, but I misunderstood him for several years. Sometimes church people give us the impression that God is a mean guy with a switch, looking to swat whoever gets out of line. I've discovered that could not be farther from the truth. I've found that God is closest to us when we need Him the most.

"Because of the Lord's great love we are not consumed, for his compassions never fail. They are new every morning; great is your faithfulness." Lamentations 3:22

CHAPTER 5

THE SENSITIVE KID

By the time my mom was 25, she was a single parent of three children, one being a newborn. Because of the abuse suffered at the hands of my dad, she made the smart decision to divorce him for our protection. She eventually married again to an older man who already had grown children of his own, who decided quickly that he wasn't up to dealing with young kids again at his age. They divorced after one year.

Then she married the man who would be the father figure that I remember the most. Don was my step dad for 13 years, from when I was 9 to 22. He rarely drank, had a good job as an engineer, and came home after work every night. Pretty good start compared to the previous two men in her life.

We soon outgrew our 2-bedroom apartment and found a home across town in a much better neighborhood that had lots of kids my age. This was the summer before my 5th grade year, and my new friends taught me how to play all kinds of sports, like football, basketball, baseball, golf and even bowling. It was a great time to be a kid in the mid 1970's, playing outdoors all the time and making friends. I couldn't wait until after school and on Saturdays to go outside and play with my new friends.

My step dad, however, had other plans for me. Our home needed many updates and repairs, and so my step dad was always starting some project on the weekends. Instead of me getting to play with my friends, Don made me help him with many home projects. Instead of playing football and basketball with my friends, I was sanding, scraping, digging and fetching tools for him.

Don hardly talked to me when we were working. I had to just wait around to fetch tools for him when he needed one. He didn't verbally teach me anything, I just had to observe what he did. It was agonizing for me.

These were my normal weekend activities, until I got a paying job at the Chinese Kitchen when I was 15. Looking back, I did learn how to use power tools, think creatively and how to do a job right the first time, which greatly benefited me as an adult. Don was impatient with me at times and had unrealistic expectations of me on occasion, but he did show me how to work, which has greatly benefitted me.

One day he was making a home-made workbench, and was trying to cut the legs all at once. My job was to hold 4 1x4's together so he could cut them all at once. Since my hands were basically too small to hold the pieces together, they slipped out of my hands when he started cutting.

He should have used a clamp to hold the pieces together, instead he cussed me out and shamed me for not being able to do the job. I was only 11 years old! He should have known it wasn't going to work. His butt-chewing scared me to death, and probably triggered the subconscious memories of my real dad's alcoholic rants.

That episode made me fearful of failing at anything as I grew older. It triggered my shame response, telling me that my best efforts would never be good enough. I became afraid of this man to say the least, and I began to wonder if all men were abusive.

Another time when I was probably 15 we were called to come to the supper table. I was in the bathroom and was the last one to sit down. Don said, "Go wash your hands young man!" I said in a defensive tone, "I just did!"

He proceeded to call me a liar, took out his belt, and began to whip me in front of everyone until my mom stopped him. She was outraged at his behavior and they got into a big nasty fight in front of us kids. My sisters ran off to their bedroom, sat on the edge of the bed, held each other and cried. But if you think I had it worse than my sisters, you might be wrong.

Years later, both of my sisters claimed that he tried to seduce them at times. I've often wondered why God allows such evil to happen to innocent children. I think it goes back to our free will as humans. I know God prevents many things, but he does allow evil to touch us at times.

When I was in college I worked at an RV dealership under the supervision of a good Godly man, who taught me a valuable lesson one day. One night at 2 am my boss's son Bryan called me up saying they needed me at work. Of course I thought he was playing a prank on me, so I laughed sarcastically.

He said, "We've had a storm out here and a lot of our fleet has been damaged." I said, "I'll be right there." There had been a small tornado, accompanied by huge hailstones that shattered roof vents and windows on just about every RV we had.

After working from 2 am to 10 am that morning, repairing what we could and covering up the rest, my boss said something I'll never forget, "Well, I guess it's too late to pray; all we can do now is give thanks."

The first thing that came to my mind was, "Give thanks? For what? You've just been put out of business!" We hadn't really been put out of business, but it felt like it at the time. As I thought about what he said, I began to understand what he was saying.

He was correct that it was too late to prevent the damage, but almost anything can be repaired or replaced. Likewise, we may not have been able to prevent storms from wrecking parts of our lives, but God is able to take the broken pieces of our lives and rebuild us like new if we will merely let him in and ask for his help. Anything can either be repaired or replaced, even our emotions and memories.

In the summer before my 8th grade year we began a 3 month long project to tear down our worn-out fence and build a new one. We could have built a new picket fence in a couple of weeks, but my step dad wanted to build a cinder block fence using materials salvaged from the famous F5 tornado that ravaged Lubbock in 1970.

It literally took us all summer long, working on the weekends, to get it finished. As much as my Mom tried to reason with him, my step dad wouldn't let us go to church at all that summer. He never went to church with us anyway, unless his mother came to visit us, at which time we suddenly became members of the Church of Christ.

It was funny to me at the time to see how scared he was of his mom. He wanted to avoid the shame he would have received from his mother if she knew he didn't attend church. I was glad my mom always took us to church to hear about the love of God and Jesus. That summer took a toll on me, because my step dad was verbally abusive at times, and he was asking a lot of a 13 year old.

My Junior High years had their share of ups and downs. I became the primary pitcher on our baseball team and went 6-1 as a starter, making the All-star team. I also won the battling title with a .471 batting average. I had a whole shelf full of trophies. I became a good pitcher by practicing with my older cousin Rodney. He was really good, and I got better by trying to keep up with him. I also enjoyed having the dream experience of winning a game with bases loaded, two outs, one run behind and me hitting a game-winning double. Two more feet and it would have been a grand slam!

In 7th grade, my best friend Terry and I won the positions as receivers on our YFL team. When we were trying out for the position, I caught everything that was thrown to me. Terry and I had spent hours and hours playing catch on our block, so we were pretty good.

After the tryout, the coach gathered the team up, but he told me to go deep for a pass. He threw a 40-yard bomb to me and I stretched out for the catch. He said in amazement, "Man, that kid has hands!" So my quarterback Mike started calling me "hands" from then on. Those were the good times.

In 8th grade, after spending the summer building that fence and skipping church, I remember one evening after supper I went into the living room, popped on the tv, sat down on the couch and just started to sob quietly. My mom came in asking me what was wrong, and all I could say was, "I don't know." 13-year-old boys can feel emotions without being able to label them.

Many mornings that year I was afraid to go to school, because I was scared and intimidated by our 8th grade football coach, who was also my social studies teacher. He was tough and intimidating, and he threatened to "nail us to the wall" if we screwed up in his class.

Most of the kids knew he was exaggerating just so we all knew he was the boss, but because of my history with men it scared the crap out of me! Some days I would literally make myself sick with fear because I had to see this guy in class and in football. Those were tough days for me.

My mom finally took me to see the school counselor one day because of my fears. He was a good man, and he gave me a few tips to get through a few more days, but he was just scratching the surface of the deep troubles that lay inside my heart. God had to intervene for me in order to snap me out of the fear cycle I was in, so he allowed me to suffer a significant back injury in football practice one day, and all at once I was out of football and away from that coach.

Well, it worked! My fear of going to school abruptly ended. God promises to make a way of escape, so we can bear up under the pressure, and I was grateful he did that for me. I did miss playing football though.

I wasn't cured though, even though God gave me relief from that situation, there were other situations that popped up later on. For example, my 8th grade English class required us to give an oral report one day, and I'd always been scared to death of those things. I would start the fear/shame cycle up again as soon as an oral report was assigned to us, so for weeks I would be in agony just thinking about it.

This time I was doing pretty good until one of my "friends" decided to make fun of me in the middle of my talk. My emotions got the best of me, and I had to sit down, because I started sobbing again. My teacher reprimanded him, and I soon regained my composure, but the damage to my reputation was done.

Word of what happened soon spread around school about me, and I became known as the "sensitive kid." How embarrassing…to be known as the sensitive kid in school by your peers! There was only one person who ever mentioned the incident to me, so I was glad that I wasn't ridiculed for crying. The kids were kind enough to never shame me for it.

I wondered why I was so sensitive to those things. Now, I look back and wonder how I survived those hard days. Maybe the fact that I was a good kid helped. Since I was a good athlete, I made male friends easily. I was also a good listener and I would laugh at everybody's jokes. That's a great way to get people to like you. Playing all kinds of sports helped me make it through those days as well, giving me a measure of confidence, which I really needed at the time.

As I entered high school, I started noticing the pretty girls all around me, and quite frankly, they started noticing me too. My personality was quiet and shy, but also gentle and kind. Back in Junior High one of my teachers wrote a very nice note on my report card saying, "Coby is kind and personable, and a joy to have in class."

That was so nice to hear from a man considering my history with other men. I had to look in the dictionary for the definition of "personable" and was very flattered by the compliment. The Lord actually blessed me with several good male teachers in high school, and that helped me to not stereotype all men as abusive. I'm glad the Lord gave me success in certain things during those years, but there were the hidden areas of my heart that would soon reveal themselves.

CHAPTER 6

SPIRITUAL AWAKENINGS

The summer before my junior year of high school I had an opportunity to go to camp with friends from church. Kerrville, Texas was a beautiful place to go, and it would be a life-changing week for me. I had asked Jesus into my heart as a 10-year-old, but I didn't really have a clue what he was like. Before then, hearing sermons just made me feel guilty that I wasn't a better person. But summer camp was so much fun playing sports, swimming, singing, looking at pretty girls and of course, the nightly meetings.

Our church, Trinity Church in Lubbock, has been a full gospel church since it was founded, and we were exposed to teachings about the Holy Spirit's role in the Christian walk. I had heard several people speaking in tongues during services, so I wasn't afraid of it at all; in fact I was very interested in finding out more about it.

As I was walking to our Wednesday evening service one of the pastors at camp caught up to me and started asking me how I was doing in my Christian walk. Luckily, some other kid came up and started a conversation with him, because I was afraid to admit that I didn't know much at all about my Christian faith, except that I'm just supposed to act right. That was all about to change.

During that Wednesday night service, Pastor Paul asked if anyone wanted to receive the baptism of the Holy Spirit. Since I was sitting close to the front, I was the first one up there. That night, several of us prayed to receive the baptism of the Holy Spirit into our lives. The next couple of hours were life-changing for me! Man, I'm tearing up just writing this down.

We began in worship to the Lord, then pastors started laying hands on our heads to receive the Holy Spirit according to the model set in scripture. Soon, I felt an incredible sensation of God's presence pour over me like a warm shower. I did say a few strange words that sounded like Chinese to me, but the presence of God's pure love was the real change.

I had never before felt so much love and acceptance in my heart and in my mind. My human spirit became alive within me because of the presence of the Holy Spirit. I suddenly felt truly alive for the first time in my life! I felt God's presence, a love for others, acceptance from God, and a huge thirst to know more of God.

I had never even opened up my Bible outside of church before, but now I wanted to read everything I could about Jesus. Speaking in tongues was interesting, but it was nothing compared to the sensation of pure love that comes from the presence of God! That was the highest of highs that I had ever experienced, and there were no negative side effects! I've never done drugs, in case you were wondering.

The rest of the night consisted of hugs, prayers, conversations and tears of joy. God visited us that night, and for me it was the beginning of that new creation spoken of in 2 Corinthians 5:17.

"Therefore, if anyone is in Christ, he is a new creation; the old has gone, the new has come."

At the end of that week, when everyone was returning home, many of us were changed. It was the beginning of hope for me. It was the promise of something better in my life, this was an awesome new feeling. The very next week I was asked to be a counselor at our elementary kids' camp, and my boss was kind enough to let me off work. I was in charge of a half dozen of the brightest young men in our church, and we had a blast! It was good for me to be involved in ministry. That week I felt the Lord's love and compassion for others, and the Lord gave me favor with the kids.

In the next months ahead I began to read as much scripture as I could, and my prayer life began to take off as well. I would come home from school, kneel down at my bed and spend time with the Lord until it was time to go to work at the Chinese Kitchen restaurant. It was a good time in my life, a time of new beginnings and new perspectives.

The youth director at Trinity called me one day and asked if I wanted to help out with the Junior High class, and I eagerly accepted. I did whatever I could do to help out, even getting the chance to lead a small Bible study for the kids. It was great getting to know the kids, but to minister and pray for the kids was my blessing.

I finally felt wanted, needed and appreciated for the first time in my life. To be used by God for His purposes was the most fulfilling experience of my life. I was also looked up to by those around me and actually experienced favor and popularity with the kids.

The prayer I prayed the most during this time period was for my step dad to get saved. It was my top priority, my #1 heart's desire for Don to get saved, experience God's love, and then apologize to all of us for the terrible things he did to us. Yes, I admit it was part altruistic, part selfish. Then I thought, we could be the happy family that I'd always wanted. Unfortunately, he was a stubborn, emotionally closed off man that thought church was just for women and children.

Anytime I would try to witness to him about the Lord he would blow me off or even ridicule me. I kept on praying and hoping for a miracle, because this was by far the deepest desire of my heart—to have a Godly father for once in my life. But as many of us know, there can be an adult male in the household, but he may not be a good and loving daddy.

When my daughter Macy was 5 she asked me, "Daddy, is God as big as you?" I laughingly replied, "No, God is way bigger than me!" Her question reminded me just how important it is for a child to have a good father, because we fathers represent God to our children.

If someone never knew their dad, they may have a hard time believing in God. If someone had a good daddy, they could easily believe in God, but if someone had a bad experience with a dad, they might think God is a mean, angry, judgmental guy that could care less about them.

My step dad did a number on me that caused me to have an improper attitude towards the Lord at times. Whenever I would ask Don a question, he would usually ignore me, as if I didn't even ask. At the time I didn't understand why he would ignore me, but I understand much better now.

The way that affected me was in my prayer times with the Lord. I was tempted at times to think that it was selfish to pray for myself. I could easily pray for the needs of others, but believing for myself was a struggle. In my subconscious I felt it wasn't okay for me to have needs. Or worse, maybe I wasn't as deserving of God's love as others were. Unresolved conflicts just pass from one relationship to another until resolved.

I know many of us tend to think this way, that God loves other people more than us, otherwise He would have given us loving parents like our friends have. I grew to resent God for failing to meet my need for a good daddy. Luckily for me, God looked beyond my resentment and continued working out His plan for me.

Satan was trying to deceive me with thoughts of rejection, and the evidence of my life seemed to support his theory. I began to think only good Christians were blessed by God, and that He really only loved the "beautiful people." I felt like a second class citizen when I looked at my circumstances, especially when I looked at my friends' lives.

Many of my church friends had great parents, and their dads went to church with them, but I didn't know that blessing personally. It was easy to believe that God had favorites, and that for some reason I didn't deserve what my friends had.

Thinking of myself as "less than" I took on the idea that I just needed to try harder at being a good Christian. I began to take on a performance mindset, seeking to do so much good that people would see me as worthy of love, and in hopes that God would see fit to love me the way He loved others.

That sounds sad, but that was what the experiences of my life had convinced me of, and that is what countless people today believe about God. Comparison is a terrible trap to fall into. Nothing good comes of it. It only makes us feel better than or less than others.

As I ministered to the kids at church I felt happy and loved by God, but when I struggled with my anger and resentments, I felt very unlovable. I thought, "As long as I do more good than bad, maybe that'll buy God's love." I promise you, this is the mindset of nearly EVERY person who attends church today. Even most pastors today talk more about "being good" than about how Jesus has already made us loveable in His eyes.

I haven't heard a "Jesus loves you" in church in years. We have no idea that Jesus has made us righteous in God's sight through His own blood, and not by our good works. I hope the Holy Spirit convinces you of how much God loves you as you read the rest of my story.

Unfortunately, the church is full of people who have only tasted of the Tree of the Knowledge of Good and Evil, and don't know how to taste of the Tree of Life. It's easier for us to believe in the idea of working for rewards, than to understand the concept that Jesus has wiped away our sins. This is one huge issue that causes us Christians to suffer needlessly in our lives. We don't go deep enough into study of scripture to see the hidden treasures of truth that are in the Bible. It's not a book of "Do's and Don'ts" it's the Book of LIFE!"

I told my kids a while back to seek out God's truth in all things, even the things they hear in church, because this is the age of deception where even Christians teach errors and false teachings. Find out for yourself what God's word actually says about you; you will be pleasantly surprised! Matthew 11:30 says His yoke is easy and His burden is light. It's so sad that churches rarely go deeper than just "How to be a better person."

So what we find in our churches and in our hearts is a religious mindset, where our righteousness depends on our performance, not on the sacrifice of Jesus. Our churches are filled with self-righteous people who are constantly judging and comparing themselves with others. Many people get turned off by supposed Christians that just don't know the freedom that comes from knowing the real Jesus.

This has happened to all of us, and I'm so sorry that it likely has happened to you. Think of it like this. There are hundreds if not thousands of Elvis Presley impersonators out there; some good, some bad. Christians are like Jesus' impersonators; some people resemble Jesus, but most don't. There's only one true Elvis, and there's only one True Jesus. We should look to Jesus, not other Christians for our example.

The Lord requires humility from us instead of our religious pride. I love this passage from Micah 6:8 that states what God demands of us.

"He has shown you, Oh man, what is good, and what the Lord requires of you; but to do justly, love mercy, and walk humbly with your God."

Nothing in that passage says, "Try your hardest to impress me, and maybe I'll let you into heaven."

NO! It just says to be fair with others, love the fact that by God's mercy our sins have been forgiven, and just humbly invite Jesus into our daily lives. Remember, in the garden of Eden Adam walked and talked with God every evening. God just wants our presence, not our sacrifices to impress him with our achievements. I hope that relieves some of your unnecessary suffering right there.

For Thanksgiving in 1981, my family met together at my Grandparents' house. My sister Rhonda and I went for a drive around the tiny little town one afternoon, just reminiscing on our lives. As we drove the dusty dirt roads of the town Rhonda said, "You know it's hard to believe you can be number one when you've always been treated like…" "Like number two?" I chirped in.

We busted out laughing at the poop reference, and it was a welcome comic relief from the "poor us" conversation. It was nice to be able to talk with someone who had the same experiences. Galatians 6:2 says,

"Share one another's burdens and so fulfill the law of Christ."

the troubles of our childhood had at least worked a sense of humor into our lives.

After graduating from Coronado HS in 1981 I started taking classes at Texas Tech. I hadn't figured out a major yet, so I just took the basics at first. My mom paid for my first semester, but I had to pay for the rest. I worked at the RV dealership 32 hours a week while taking a full load at Tech. My prayer times were focused on what career the Lord wanted me to pursue, but I wasn't getting any clear messages at first.

One day during my first semester as I was praying, the Lord sent me the thought that I should read Isaiah 45. As I began to read the first few verses it sounded interesting, but I didn't quite get the message. I came to understand years later that it was a prophetic message from the Lord, telling me what He was about to do in my life.

"I will go before you and will level the mountains: I will break down gates of bronze and cut through bars of iron. I will give you the treasures of darkness, riches stored in secret places, so that you may know that I am the Lord, the God of Israel, who calls you by name." Isaiah 45:2-3

Through the next decade, the Lord would place me in situations to help me discover what was buried in my subconscious and help me to process as an adult, the things I had taken on as a child. He would speak words of deliverance to me during the darkest times of my life. These words would be the treasures of darkness, the hidden riches of revelation, only to be found through my sufferings. God knew what I needed to hear, and He was preparing my heart to receive his truth.

CHAPTER 7

THE GREAT DEPRESSION

By the summer of 1982 my time of ministry to the kids was in full swing. We were just loading up the buses for the best week of the year... summer camp! This year we were going to the beautiful mountains of Colorado. The scenery was breathtaking and we had speakers at camp that year.

One guest speaker, Darryl, was very popular with the kids, and they were always begging for his attention. He seemed very sensitive to the Holy Spirit, and was often giving prophetic words of encouragement to the kids. One day during our free time, Darryl caught a moment alone with me, and we began to talk. He looked at me with concern and said, "You've been hurt by your father, haven't you?"

I was taken by surprise at his words, wondering how a complete stranger could know something so personal about me. "Yes sir." was all I remember saying back. Suddenly, a group of kids found us and reported that someone needed Darryl's help, so off he went.

We didn't get to finish our talk, needless to say, and I was left standing there with a dumb look on my face. The reality of his words hit me with a force, and I was once again reminded of my family troubles. My countenance changed, and that revelation felt like a kick in the gut, and suddenly I was reminded that I had a broken heart deep inside me.

Darryl never got back to me to give encouragement or counsel, and I just didn't handle that information well. In the next hour or so many of those old fears and feelings came rushing back into my mind. The pain that had been buried under the false confidence of doing good works came back for a visit.

When camp was over and I returned home, my mom could tell right away that something was wrong. "Why are you so depressed? What happened?" she asked. "I don't know." was all I could say. For weeks and weeks I walked around like a zombie, crushed under the realization that I had a lot of buried wounds. Satan was having fun tormenting me with thoughts like…

1) You're damaged goods

2) You're not worthy of love from anyone

3) You'll never get over your broken heart

4) Your future will be as bad as your past

5) And the worst lie of all–God doesn't really love you

Those were horrible, empty days and I'm glad I don't remember too much of those days now. Things at home were not good for my sisters either. I was going to church, hanging out with friends, going to school and working. I was rarely at home except to sleep and eat. My step dad was a strange guy, but I never dreamed he would do what he did to my sisters.

One day as we came home from church Rhonda was very upset. She told us Don came into her bedroom that morning stark naked. She screamed and ran out. Then my younger sister Kim confessed to the same experience at an earlier time. Mother was FURIOUS! I was shocked!

Within the week Don moved out of the house and into an apartment. When the divorce was finalized, I was devastated! Not only did this end their marriage, but it also destroyed my dreams that Don would become my Christian dad. All I ever wanted, all I asked of the Lord, was to have a dad that would love me the right way, and this absolutely crushed my heart.

A deep depression began to settle over me, and my heart began to close off to everyone, including God. My sisters and I experienced the same upbringing, but we all dealt with our pain in different ways. Since I had a melancholy personality I just turned quiet and inwards. I wondered if it was my fault somehow, and I became very angry with God. Why did God not answer my prayers? Shame told me it was my fault.

One night soon after the divorce I had a terrible dream. I dreamt I was fighting someone and a poisonous snake attacked me from behind, clenching onto my back just below my left shoulder blade. When I woke up my back was killing me in that very spot. This was a demonic attack, allowed by my anger towards God.

When we are hurt on any of our three parts (body, soul or spirit) it often will affect the other two parts of us at the same time. Physical infirmities can come on us as a result of emotional trauma. My spiritual pain of anger towards God was manifesting in emotional torment and now in physical pain on my back.

In the weeks ahead, when I tried to pray, it just ended up with me shouting my anger towards God. And when my feelings of emotional torment came back up, that snake bite would be felt once again on my back! At the time I didn't have enough understanding about spiritual warfare to know that this was a demonic attack. Creepy! This was the worst time in my life, because I had lost my trust in God. I was convinced that I was cursed, and the spirit of shame told me I would never be loved.

The religious part of me still provided for a regular prayer life, but now my prayers were heartless and dull. I called them token prayers because they all sounded the same… lifeless and empty. "Lord, please help me through this day…blah, blah, blah" was about all I could muster.

Then one day while praying, I asked the Lord if there was anything he wanted to say to me. We forget that prayer was meant to be a conversation between God and us. Anyway, the Lord had something to show me that day.

Listening to the Lord with my eyes closed, I heard the sound of pottery breaking, then a vision of people standing around in a circle. They seemed to be looking at the broken pieces with concern, saying, "It's broken, can't be fixed. Too bad." Then someone entered the circle, knelt down and began to pick up the pieces. Then, the vision was over. I opened my eyes, looked around the room and thought, "Well, that was strange." I wondered what that vision meant. About a month later I got the answer.

It was the winter of 1983. The college group and the singles' groups from church were heading to a ski retreat together. It had been a couple of months since my parents' divorce, and somehow I got stuck riding on the singles' bus. While we stopped for a bathroom break along the way, people began filing off the bus.

I was sitting in a window seat close to the front, just thinking about my parents' divorce, when I just started to cry. I tried not to let anyone see me, but the singles' pastor noticed me, sat down by me and asked what was wrong. I began to cry harder and louder as he began to pray for me.

After a minute I looked up and out the window to see several people standing outside in a circle, looking up at me wondering what could possibly be wrong. Just then the Lord reminded me of that vision I had, and He spoke to my thoughts saying, "Coby, I can heal your broken heart. The man that picked up the broken pieces was Jesus, and we are going to put you back together again, piece by piece." That showed me that God forgave me for my angry words towards him, and was still going to work out His good plan for my life. This was an encouraging sign for me.

I want to interrupt my story for a second and share one thing that happens when we give our hearts to Jesus. To us, that salvation prayer is just something we say to become a Christian, but it is much more binding and significant to the Lord. At that time He actually makes a solemn and lasting covenant with us to NEVER LEAVE US and NEVER FORSAKE US, and He begins to work out His divine plan to heal us and set us free. As long as we acknowledge Him in our lives, He will never let go of us.

He doesn't change his mind when we get upset and falsely accuse Him of doing wrong. He sees past it, because our anger has already been forgiven at the cross of Jesus. We have no idea how much God goes out of his way to take care of us on a daily basis, even when we can ignore Him for days on end. HE IS FAITHFUL ALWAYS, even when we are not.

In the days ahead my heart began to open up a little bit, even though I was still angry and disappointed with God. I was still going to college and working at the RV dealership. At my job I was usually the first one to get there. I would unlock the RVs and turn the heat on in the shop.

One particular morning I saw a beautiful rainbow in the eastern sky where it had been raining. While unlocking the RVs I started rehearsing the verse in the Bible that says the rainbow is God's promise to never again flood the entire earth. At that very moment the Lord spoke very clearly to my spirit, saying, "Coby, if you will come back to me with all of your heart, I promise you will never again have floods of sorrow in your life."

Tears began streaming down my face as I felt the sweet presence of God fall on me like that day at summer camp years before. It was as if God got off his throne in heaven, lifted my face up with his hands, and spoke directly into my heart.

It's impossible to describe the sensation of the presence of God, except to say it is pure love and peace. The closest thing I can compare it to is the emotional equivalent of a warm shower on a cold winter day, completely peaceful and soothing. Take a moment and imagine God or Jesus coming into your room, hugging you and telling you He loves you no matter how others have treated you. It's the safest and sweetest place to be...in His presence.

As you might imagine, this event had a profound effect on me. I could hardly concentrate at work that day, but it was all good. God had visited me that day! Experiences with God change our lives forever, and He was reaching out to me in miraculous ways. My heart was opening back up to the Lord more and more because of His kindness to me.

CHAPTER 8

PALESTINE

In the last few months of 1983, God began to give me more visions during my prayer times. Let me add here that visions are not spooky, scary images, at least not visions from the Holy Spirit. They are very similar to our daydreams, but only they are daydreams from God's Spirit. It is one of the ways God speaks to us.

In his book The Fourth Dimension, Dr. Paul Youngi Cho says that dreams and visions are the language of the Holy Spirit. Since I have been more of a visual learner than an auditory learner, the Lord was generous to reveal specific things to me by way of His visions.

God would speak basic life principles through reading the Bible, but special direction through those visions. One recurring vision was of me taking a long road trip in my 1977 Camaro. Back then I enjoyed listening to the Chariots of Fire album from Vangelis, and I had one of those car trip visions while listening to Abraham's Theme. Such a beautiful song. I couldn't imagine where I was going, but the visions intrigued me nonetheless.

I stayed active in youth ministry at church, when one day a new opportunity came up. The Junior High pastor was moving to be an associate pastor in a town in east Texas called Palestine. Pastor Bryan and his wife Kim asked me and my friend Warren to come along and help out with the youth group there.

Warren agreed to go immediately; he couldn't wait to get out of Lubbock. I had to think about it for a while. After praying about it, and asking some trusted people what they thought, I was convinced that it was God's will for my life. I soon realized this was the trip that the Lord had been showing me about in my prayers and dreams.

For most of my life I'd lived in the same city, same surroundings and same expectations about life. The Lord was about to introduce me to a new way of thinking about life, about myself and about Him. Warren and I drove to Palestine in the winter of 1984. He had already been there and dropped off some of his personal effects the week before.

We were moving into an old 2-story Victorian house that had been turned into a quadruplex. When we got there it was very cold, and we discovered that Warren had left the bathtub full of water and it had frozen solid! We had a good laugh over that! After we turned the heat on in the apartment, unpacked our stuff and melted the tub down, we took a drive around town.

Palestine Texas was a beautiful place, even in the winter. There were trees as high as the sky it seemed, especially since we had come from the flatlands of West Texas. Palestine was a small town of about 12,000 and unlike Lubbock, there wasn't a single road that didn't twist, curve, or rise and fall. There was even one road they called "roller coaster road." I had a little too much fun on that road one day, and had to get my exhaust replaced on my Camaro. Oops! It was exciting for us to be in a new place, with new adventures ahead.

The next day as we arrived at our new church, we got our first exposure to that famous southern hospitality! Warren and I were introduced to the congregation of 300 as the new youth group associates, and not 5 minutes after the service, had already been invited to someone's home for lunch. A home cooked meal with sweet, loving people. I could get used to this!

In the days to come we came to meet many of the people from church and the kids in the youth group. We were excited to be there and they were excited to have us. Sometimes when you move to a new place where nobody knows you, you get treated with more respect than you think you deserve. We were treated like royalty, and everyone wanted to get to know us.

There were about 3 families in particular that took me under their wings, and I can't remember a single Sunday afternoon that I wasn't invited to join one of those families for lunch. It was usually a gathering of at least 2 or more families that would eat and fellowship together, and they treated me like family. At 21 years of age, the Lord was placing me in a loving environment in order to show me that life can change for the better, and I was so grateful for God's kindness to reach out to me in such wonderful ways.

One particular Sunday about 20 people gathered at Dick and Rose's home; the women preparing the feast and the men watching the Dallas Cowboys on tv. I had become well acquainted with many of the people there, many of them having been a true blessing to me in some manner. But for some reason, I just felt all alone. I felt disconnected with everyone, a feeling that I was familiar with in times past.

Something must have triggered feelings of rejection and the thought that I didn't belong there. As I sat quietly, watching the game, the Lord spoke quietly in my thoughts. He said, "Coby why are you so down? Look around and show me one person who hasn't shown you love and acceptance." I couldn't find anyone.

God has a way of making a point. I couldn't name one person there who had rejected me or been anything but kind to me. Then it began to dawn on me, these people weren't the source of my loneliness. So where did this feeling come from?

God has given us the gift of emotions to help us interpret and enjoy life. But sometimes we misunderstand what our emotions are trying to tell us. Emotions have no agenda; they just reveal if an experience is happy or sad, generally speaking. Our mind can trick us into believing a lie if our emotional response is painful. If a certain painful emotion repeats itself, there may be a wound that needs to be tended to. My feeling of loneliness and rejection had nothing to do with the people in that home, it was telling me there was a wound in my past that needed to be tended to.

One reason God sent me to this church was to be pastored by a great man named Ron MacIntosh, who the Lord used as an instrument in my spiritual growth. Ron preached a message of righteousness that I'd never heard before in any church. He preached about our power, our authority as believers, and our condition of being righteous in God's eyes through Jesus. The first time I heard him state that we were righteous in God's eyes it sounded like heresy. I'd always been to churches that told us we are all sinners that needed to become better people.

I had never heard about spiritual warfare, or the fact that Satan and his demons were out to destroy people with lies and deception. I had just assumed the devil was in hell torturing all the bad guys. Pastor Ron's sermons were powerful and insightful to me and I learned a lot through his teaching.

He stated many times that believers were already righteous in God's eyes because of the sacrifice of Jesus on the cross. I thought a righteous person was someone like Moses or Paul the Apostle, but now Ron was telling me that "I" was also righteous? That was a new concept for sure. How could I be considered righteous when there was so much wrong with me?

The reason I couldn't comprehend God's love for me was because that space had already been occupied by the belief that I was unlovable. My daddy's treatment of me had convinced my subconscious that there was something unlovable about me. God was starting to confront that lie with His truth. At this juncture I was introduced to one of the most powerful and life-changing verses of the Bible.

"We demolish arguments and every pretension that sets itself up against the knowledge of God, and we take captive every thought to make it obedient to Christ." 2 Corinthians 10: 5-6

It was easy for me to believe the lies trapped in my soul because of the body of evidence of my life experiences. It was easy to believe God was mad at me for all of the sins of my heart; the anger, jealousy, bitterness and unforgiveness. Preachers had told me for years that Christians are supposed to love everybody, but I wasn't always loving, in fact, I even hated some people!

Satan had lied to me from childhood about who I was and about what I could expect out of life. I was trying hard to buy God's love by doing good works for Him, but the good feelings were all short-lived. Everybody seemed to have more money, a better car, a home with a good mom and dad, and just an easier life than I had. I felt left out and singled out to pay for my sins and the sins of others.

Knowing that my family life was different from others made me feel inferior, as if God had forgotten about me, or that God was just being unfair to me. God's word says it's a sin to compare your life to others' because it only leads to one of two things, either pride or envy. God says to be content where we are and with what we have, even as we work to grow in wealth and wisdom. The 10th commandment says we should not covet what our neighbor has, or hate them for their success. I really struggled with jealousy of others and feelings that God was being unfair to me.

During my time in Palestine I began to write in a journal, as suggested by Pastor Ron. Our church was learning how to have quiet times with the Lord, including writing down our prayers and any answers to prayer we had received. So I began to write down my thoughts and prayers, and the things God was teaching me along the way.

This was very helpful for me; it helped me organize my thoughts and feelings about everything, and it kept me focused on what the Lord was doing in my heart. I highly recommend it, and I also recommend you find a strong, trustworthy friend to help talk things out with.

There was a sweet girl in our youth group that I usually gave a ride home to, since her parents did not attend church with her. Lexie and I developed a great friendship as we would sit outside her house and literally talk for hours about what each of us was dealing with.

As we explored the deep meanings of life, we discovered that we came up with our own answers just by being allowed to talk it out. It was so therapeutic for both of us, and I pray that you will also find a kind soul to listen to you process your thoughts and feelings. Then hopefully as you heal, you can become that person for your friends in turn.

One of the new teachings we had was about breaking down strongholds of Satan in our lives. We were taught to bind the spirits of darkness and to loose the Holy Spirit of God to heal and set us free from lies and deceptions. Warren and I, and sometimes another friend, would come over to our apartment and pray. We would search our hearts for any possible sin or evil spirit that might be oppressing us.

That was an exhausting time for me, because we would sometimes stay up till 2 am praying, and I had to be at work at 6 am the next morning. We may have been taking things a little extreme there, but we were learning. There is not an evil spirit behind every challenge we face, sometimes it's just our own negative thoughts that are tormenting us.

Some strongholds are spiritual and some are soulish. The spiritual ones have to be addressed in prayer in the authority of Jesus. The soulish ones can usually just be talked out as we allow ourselves to express our feelings. Sometimes they can pass just by crying it out. Men are allowed to cry when they need to. It won't turn you into a sissy, trust me. It did the exact opposite for me.

Men, think of it in this way. We pride ourselves in not being afraid of anything, right? But most men are afraid of their own emotions, especially the sad ones. Think of those sad emotions as a bully. A real man stands up and faces his bullies, right? Then it is very manly to face your emotions and listen to what they are telling you. If you run away and ignore those bullies, they will chase you and torment you again.

If you suppress or ignore your emotions, the ones that continue to pop up in your soul, then you are actually betraying yourself. Your soul is trying to get you to notice something that needs to be addressed. If we listen to our emotions, and discover what they are trying to tell us, we can make whatever adjustment is needed, and those emotions will stop bugging us. If we ignore our promptings, they will continue to bug us.

So be brave; listen to your heart and you will find a way to resolve the issue. Allow yourself to feel the disappointment, the shame or whatever it is. If you face those emotions and let yourself feel them, they will be satisfied and usually go away. God gave us feelings for a reason. Begin to listen to your feelings and let them pass through you, then you will really become a bad-ass that's able to face anything! With every fear we face, we become more confident and healthier.

Here's an example. Let's say your wife is complaining that you golf too much and are not helping her with the house enough. Do you argue with her, or do you honestly think about it? If you just try to get her to shut up, without determining if she has a valid point, then you will be bothered with guilty feelings every time you go golfing.

If you stop and judge for yourself, even get advice from a trusted friend, then you can face the issue. Once you figure out if you really are being selfish or not, you can change and find a balance, or calmly tell your wife you need some time for yourself. I remember a season when I was working so much the Lord actually called me on it and said, "Why are you working so hard? Why don't you take some time and go golfing?" I was working 6-7 days a week and hadn't golfed in months. A lot of men are under the assumption that they have to work really hard all the time. Balance is much healthier.

CHAPTER 9

THE ROOT OF REJECTION

The battle for my soul was on, and in full swing. Many tears were shed and a few strongholds were broken, beginning with the stronghold of pride. The first thing the Lord had me address was the spirit of pride that had a subtle but strong hold in my heart. Remember in chapter 3 discussing the baseline of shame that we all suffer from? Well the coping mechanism of choice seems to be to put on a shield of pride, hoping to protect our hearts from getting hurt again.

The only problem with taking on pride is that it closes off our hearts; nothing gets in and nothing gets out. The Spirit of God can't work in our hearts when we are covering it up with the band-aid of pride. This type of pride manifests itself as defensiveness. When we try to confront someone about something, and they get defensive… that's their pride talking. The Bible says God resists the proud, but gives grace to the humble.

When a dog gets wounded it will retreat to a safe place to lick its wounds and soothe himself. If anyone gets close to him in this condition he will bark fiercely to chase the intruder away. Humans can't hide away. We have to continue living and interacting with the world, so we just pretend we didn't get hurt, or act like it didn't bother us. We cover up the wound with false pride.

We've all done this to some extent, but we have to eventually come to grips with our pain and somehow process it, or it will continue to bother us. If we don't allow ourselves to process the emotions we feel, they will remain in our minds, emotions and even our bodies, like my snake bite sensation.

Unfortunately, I had no clue how to process my emotions and "cast my cares on the Lord" like the Word suggests. But like I stated in the first chapter, God created us with the ability to grow, to learn, to seek wisdom and solve problems. But before we feel safe enough to ask for help, we have to let go of the false security of pride. Pride comes before a fall, but humility comes before honor.

The Lord helped me take authority over the stronghold of pride and tell it to leave me in the name of Jesus, and it did! Jesus gives us power over the enemy when we address the enemy in Jesus' name and authority. Awesome! The devil has no power over or right to a believer, unless we allow him to. All we have to do is resist him, and he has to flee.

"Submit yourselves then to God. Resist the devil, and he will flee from you. Draw near to God and He will draw near to you." James 4:7-8

Since I was praying and self-reflecting so much, the Lord spoke to me often at this time. One night I was voicing some frustration to the Lord over what seemed like a mountain of problems I was discovering. Remember, a lot of this stuff was buried in my subconscious from childhood, so it was a little overwhelming to realize how much junk was being resurfaced.

Our problems are overwhelming if we think it's our job to fix ourselves, but it's actually God's job to change us. It's our job to ask for help, but God actually changes us. We just have to be still, listen and allow Him to speak truth and life to us. As Christians, our sins have been removed from us by the sacrifice of Jesus on the cross, so now He just wants to expose and correct the thoughts and beliefs that are keeping us from believing that He loves us. He said, "Coby, your problems don't worry me at all. I know what I'm doing in your life, and we are making progress. Don't give up and don't be afraid." He was so kind to reveal Himself to me.

The Christian life is very different from the ways of the world. The world's wisdom says to push your way through until you get what you want, no matter who you have to hurt in the process. God calls us His sheep, and pretty much all sheep do is listen to the voice of the shepherd, go where his staff directs them and EAT!

We don't have to agonize over anything because He is caring for us. All we have to do is just listen, obey and enjoy His presence. Don't let preachers tell you God needs your help to save the world. That is an unnecessary burden that religious people place on us. Yes, God will use us, but He has already prepared those good works in advance. We just have to stay close to the Lord and be ready when those opportunities arise.

In the next few days God showed me something profound about my situation. He showed me that all of my relationship problems were really just caused by one root issue… a root of rejection.

He gave me a word picture about it to help me understand. He showed me a picture of my significant relationships of the past as tree branches, springing from one big root underground. He was showing me that we really only had to focus on the root of the problem, not all of the branches. What a relief!

Just a thought here: We as Christians tend to make our walk of faith so complicated, but the Lord is so simple in how He interacts with us. He actually wants to simplify our lives, not complicate them. Most psychologists tend to deal with clients' behavior, but the Lord speaks to the matters of the heart, the root issues that affect our behavior.

Our behaviors don't just appear like animal instincts. There is a pattern or cycle of behavior that I've been taught that explains this. First we are exposed to a stimulus, an experience of words or actions, which elicits a feeling or an emotion. If we feel this specific emotion repeatedly, it elicits a thought. Rehearsing that thought then leads to the development of a belief about life. It is our beliefs about certain life experiences that then drive our behavior.

Focusing only on behavior is skipping a few important steps. And I'll go further to say we can't just pray away our insecurities as if it's just a demon. We have to examine the feelings, thoughts and false beliefs so that the pain will leave us. Casting out a demon will correct a spiritual stronghold, but we also must address the soul wounds.

Most Christians would rather pray the pain away than to face the issues and resolve them with truth. God will provide us many chances to face our fears, and we can temporarily pray the fear away, but we eventually will need to address the hidden wound so the pain will be resolved. This is the place where Jesus becomes real to us. As we engage Jesus in conversation about our feelings, He reveals the memories, the lies and then the truth to us, so we can replace the false belief with the truth.

This is why scripture tells us to take every thought captive, and compare it to what God says about us as His children. I also want to add here that not every thought that comes into your mind is from you. The Holy Spirit speaks to you through your thoughts, you have your own thoughts and evil spirits can also give you thoughts.

God gives us the power, the right and the duty to filter out every thought that comes into our head. The only way to know which thoughts are true and which are lies is to study the Word of God. Don't just take someone's word for granted, even if they are an authority figure. I'll warn you here that the world's wisdom is based on how to manipulate others, but the wisdom from God is based on love.

Don't even believe everything in this book if you don't agree with me. I'm certainly not the expert on any of this. GO TO THE WORD OF GOD for the truth! Find out for yourself what God thinks and says about you. Most Christians only know God from what they hear a preacher say, and not all preachers have a good understanding of the kind and generous nature of God. Church is merely an introduction to God; there is more buried treasure in the Bible just waiting to be found than you can imagine. Listen to this passage of scripture…

*"The law of the Lord is perfect, **reviving the soul.***

*The statutes of the Lord are trustworthy, **making wise the simple.***

*The precepts of the Lord are right, **giving joy to the heart.***

*The commands of the Lord are radiant, **giving light to the eyes.***

*The fear of the Lord is pure, **enduring forever.***

*The ordinances of the lord are **sure and altogether righteous.***

*They are **more precious than gold**, than much pure gold.*

*By them your servant is **warned.***

*In keeping them there is **great reward.***"Psalm 19:7-11

The Word of God has also been described as water that cleanses the soul and quenches our thirst. The Lord had revealed to me that I had a root of rejection in my heart since childhood, and it was a big, fat root and it was deep. I've pulled up a million weeds in my lifetime, and some were so big I had to water the ground around them before I could pull them out.

The Lord was watering the ground around my root of rejection by revealing his word to me, teaching me about the authority I had in Jesus, and by putting me in a safe place with caring people. Palestine was a safe place for me to soften up the hard places of my heart and I'm so grateful He sent me there.

CHAPTER 10

BREAKING THE CHAINS

So there I was; in a new town, with new friends, new opportunities and new experiences. While I had many great, exciting times in Palestine, there were also some very lonely times. In the fall of 1984, we had a rainstorm that lasted for 2 solid weeks! It must have been hurricane season. Being from Lubbock, I was not used to so much rain. I thought it would never end.

My roommate had gone back to Lubbock for a visit during the second week of the storm. So not only was I alone, I couldn't even work at my construction job because it was so muddy. I found myself bored, lonely, broke and I was an easy target for depression. Satan knew this was his opportunity to get to me.

Charles Stanley was like a spiritual father to me, even though I never met him. He had a regular piece of advice, warning us to never get too hungry, too angry, too lonely or too tired, because if we did, we would be ripe for temptation. I was very lonely and frustrated at this point, and Satan ramped up the torment. He took the opportunity to tell me that I wasn't going to ever get over my problems, so I might as well quit trying.

I remember on Wednesday of that second week laying on the floor, praying that God would make Satan go away and quit bothering me. I felt like a little child, and I was acting like one. Where was God now, and why was He letting Satan attack me?

The Lord mercifully spoke to my spirit, "Coby, you are going to have to learn to fight...or you will die." That's all he said to me. It was said in a loving way, but this was a little more coach-like. The Lord was not shaming me in His tone, but He was giving me a stern warning. Fortunately, God convicts us without shaming or condemning us.

The Lord had been training and teaching me for months on how to fight the enemy, but at this point I had dropped my guard and let my emotions take over my thoughts once again. God was saying to me, "Look, I've given you the weapons of warfare against Satan, fed you the truth that I love you in countless ways; now it's time for you to stand up for yourself and fight the lies. Who are you going to agree with, Satan or Me?"

Well, it was gut check time for me. Was I going to follow through with my training, or was I going to give up and die? Somehow I managed to say a timid prayer of resistance against Satan, which had no power until I said, "In the name of Jesus." Well, it worked!

Sometimes the only thing we can speak in our defense is the name of Jesus, and it is probably the most important thing we can pray. Satan had to leave my presence because I used the authority of Jesus' name. Think about this for a moment. I was very weak, but the name of Jesus alone rescued me. "In Him all things hold together."

When you are in a weakened state, and you feel the attack of Satan, CALL on Jesus and/or a trusted friend. Don't let the enemy run over you. We need each other, but if nobody is available, call out to Jesus. He WILL hear you and come to you.

"For the eyes of the Lord roam to and fro throughout the whole earth, looking to show himself strong in the behalf of those whose hearts are perfect towards Him." 2 Chronicles 16:9.

I love that verse! But don't let the part about having a perfect heart scare you. A perfect heart in God's mind is the heart of a child, who brings all his broken toys to his daddy to fix. As we get older, we forget the childlike innocence of trusting someone older and wiser than us. No matter how old we get, we are encouraged to come to God with childlike faith.

Well, after two weeks the rain ended, but it was still too wet to work. One of the men from church knew I was at home alone and bored, so he invited me to go with him to check out a deer lease.

When we got to the lease, my friend Phil opened up his glovebox and retrieved a small handgun. I couldn't imagine why he needed a gun at this point, we were just checking for tracks. We found several deer tracks and decided this was a good place to hunt when it dried out a bit.

Another lonely dreary week went by and by Friday, my defenses were down again. It seemed like all of God's kindness, miracles and visions couldn't chase away my deep feelings of loneliness. I was sinking into a deep bout of depression, like the ones I had known over the past year.

At just before noon that Friday, I became overwhelmed with my inability to handle the loneliness in my heart. I decided at that point that I was done. I was through trying to fight this monster inside me. My heart was about to explode inside my chest from the pressure, and I just wanted the fight to be over. Several times in my life I've experienced great darkness right before a significant breakthrough. This was a very dark day for me.

In that instant, I remembered Phil's gun in the glovebox of his truck. Just then an eerie peace came over me…it comforted me to know that I had a way to end this suffering and torment that I had been through for 21 years. At last I was going to be free from the pain! I knew my heart could not take another day of the hell that had become my life.

Calmly, I began to walk to the door of my apartment to leave. As my hand touched the doorknob, the phone rang. The ringing of the phone angered me, because it snapped me out of the trance I was in. After 3 or 4 rings I decided to answer it.

It was my friend Dick House, inviting me to go to the lake with him and his son Ricky. Being the people pleaser that I had always been, I said, "Sure, I'll meet y'all out there after a while." But I didn't know if I would ever show up…

I got in my car and drove over to Phil and Patsy's house to get the gun. Upon arriving, neither Phil nor his pickup was there, but I rang the doorbell anyway. Patsy opened the door and invited me in, and within 15 seconds I was pouring crocodile tears all over her beautiful hardwood floor!

Patsy was caught off guard, but just her presence was enough to calm me down enough to talk. I don't remember what I told her, but I finally said, "It's okay. I'll be alright. Thank you." I ended up at the lake with Dick and Ricky, but I was a zombie! It was a good thing Dick was not a big talker, because I couldn't carry on a conversation at this point. I felt so dead inside.

That evening was our regular time to meet for the singles' fellowship, and I was glad to have somewhere to go. Our singles' leader Gary was a Godly man who I'd talked to many times about my life. After Gary gave a short message, he opened the floor up for prayer requests, and I was the first to raise my hand.

I started to share, but ended up just sobbing, "I need help." Gary called me over to the center of the room; everyone laid hands on me and began to pray. Gary had an idea of what was bothering me, and since I couldn't communicate through the tears, he began to pray aloud.

At one point Gary said, "Coby, I want you to repeat after me." He began to pray a prayer of forgiveness for my 3 dads, which I was able to follow along with, until he said, "...and I forgive my dads for what they did to me..." Gary waited for me to repeat the words, but I just couldn't say them, all I could do was cry even harder. My heart was bursting from the weight of years of disappointment and pain.

This was a prayer that I didn't want to repeat. I had no desire to forgive those jerks, but at the same time I knew I had to, or my heart would continue to bear the pain. Gary repeated the lines again and said, "Coby I know you can do it; just repeat the words." After a few seconds of silence, "And I forgive my dads for what they put me through..." passed through my quivering lips.

Suddenly, through all of the tears and blubbering, I felt something amazing happen, physically, emotionally and spiritually. The physical sensation of chains falling off my back was accompanied by a sense of freedom in my spirit. Something very profound was happening deep within my being.

Just like my rainbow experience, I felt the presence of God pour over me like another warm shower. God spoke very clearly to me at that moment, "Coby, let those men go. I'll be your father from now on." I don't know how long we all prayed, but I didn't want that moment to end. The Lord of all creation, the maker of heaven and earth, wanted to be MY Father? I had never even thought about that, or dreamed it was possible!

I didn't fully understand what had taken place, but I knew something was different inside. I felt a tremendous weight fall off me. God, through Gary, helped me pray the hardest prayer of my life. The prayer that had to be prayed out loud in order for me to begin healing from the wounds of the past.

Years later I can honestly say that one of the changes that occurred was...I have never been shackled again by the chains of depression! Oh, I've had the temporary setbacks of depression like we all do from time to time, but nothing that lasted for more than a day or two. And I never again felt that snake bite on my back to this day! Thank you Jesus! Thank you Lord, for using Gary to help me in this dark time in my life.

CHAPTER 11

BEGINNING TO HEAL

Later that night, and for the next several days, God spoke to me often. Looking back through my journal, I see that on December 18, 1984 God spoke to me a strong word about being afraid. He said, "Never be afraid that I will leave you, or stop loving you or stop looking out for you." He said if I ever had any more fears like that, to just let it motivate me to spend time with Him in prayer, so that I can begin to trust Him.

He said it would take time for me to develop trust in Him, but if fear comes in, I must rebuke it and cast it out in the name of Jesus. He said, "Don't back down to fear, but stand up to it in the name of Jesus and don't give up until it leaves." This word is for every believer, not just me. We have authority to tell fear to leave us! Awesome!

Many of my prayer times in those days were spent listening to God, and what he kept telling me was, "Don't be afraid. I love you. I'm here for you." I've heard someone say that there are exactly 365 times in the Bible that God said, "Fear not." That wouldn't surprise me, because it seemed that's what He was telling me on a daily basis.

When I prayed that prayer of forgiveness, that set me free in my spirit and in my body, but I would have to walk out the journey of restoring my soulish wounds. Remember, I did not want to say that prayer. I didn't FEEL forgiveness for my dads, but the obedient act of speaking forgiveness out loud broke the spiritual stronghold.

"The spirit of a man will sustain him in infirmity, but a wounded spirit, who can bear?" Proverbs 18:14

The Lord kindly removed the physical manifestations of my bitterness at that time as well. My prayer of forgiveness set things right in my relationship with God so that He now had permission through the Spirit to begin the healing of my mind and emotions. There are spiritual laws that most certainly affect our physical world. We also see here that you don't have to FEEL forgiveness in order to engage forgiveness in the Spirit realm. We just have to be willing to obey, then He provides the power to change.

That is really good news for Christians! That is how God can forgive OUR sins while we are still struggling with sin. We are forgiven of our sins through faith in Jesus, while we still sin in our body and soul. As long as we wear these human body suits, we are going to sin, but through Jesus, God has taken the penalty of sin and the power of sin off of us. Our spirit, which is the eternal part of us, will now live forever, while the body will eventually wear out over time and die.

Thank God the Spirit realm rules over the natural realm! We can trust in God's love and acceptance of us even when we know we still sin. God no longer sees our sin, instead He sees the blood of Jesus that now covers our sins. We have now been redeemed back to the proper relationship with God that Adam and Eve had before they sinned. We can now talk to God freely at any time of the day or night.

When we ask Jesus to forgive our sins and come into our hearts… He does! He comes to make a home for Himself in us. We become a temple of the Holy Spirit. Before Jesus died, He told his disciples He would send the Holy Spirit to them to be with them forever, to comfort them and remind them of everything He told them. The Father, the Son and the Holy Spirit are all aspects of God that have specific roles, but all work in unity to fulfill the great plan of God.

There is a verse in the New Testament that says we suffer torment when we hold unforgiveness towards another. I was most certainly tormented by my unforgiveness towards my dads, to the point of wanting to commit suicide. Dropping my pride and speaking forgiveness to my dads began the healing process.

Around this time a good friend gave me a book called Hinds Feet on High Places (by Hannah Hurnard) which taught me some important perspectives about suffering. The book is an allegory about a family of hinds (deer) that lived in a valley next to tall mountains. The main character was named Much Afraid, the smallest member of her family, the family of Fearings, and was somewhat crippled.

I began to identify with this character immediately, and I became hooked on reading the book. This book was a God-send, because it helped explain what God was doing in my heart at this point in my life. Thank you, Vanessa, for listening to the Lord and being willing to give me that book. I love how God uses other people to help us in our journey.

The crippled hind deer Much Afraid was stuck in the low places of the valley, where predators could easily attack and eat the weaker animals. The Good Shepherd challenged her to climb up to the high places where he lived, where it was safe from the coyotes and other predators. Her own fears and the negativity of her family convinced her she could never make the journey.

The part of the story that intrigued me was the companions that the Good Shepherd promised to give Much Afraid to help her make the trip. Much Afraid was excited that she would have two companions to help her make the trip, and I was also very interested to know who they were. I knew her companions would also be my companions from this point on in my own journey to the High Places of the Lord.

As I turned the page, I began to read about two large ominous figures in holocaust cloaks. That wasn't what I was expecting to read about, but I read on. The companions sent by the Good Shepherd to assist her (and me) were none other than Sorrow and Suffering! My hot tears began to drop onto the pages of this awful book!

"NO!! Why did it have to be THOSE GUYS?" I asked God. Haven't I already had enough sorrow and suffering in my life? Now these guys have been appointed by God to chase me again? I wasn't sure I wanted to continue reading that terrible book. At the time I couldn't imagine what those two guys could possibly do to help with her journey or with mine.

Hannah Hurnard goes into great detail explaining the way we grow and learn best from the darkest times and the greatest challenges of our lives. I continued reading the entire book and it was wonderful! I highly recommend it.

I will certainly talk more about the benefits of facing the sorrows and sufferings of our lives, instead of running away from them. There is no escaping hurts and disappointments in this life, so we may as well learn how to benefit from them. I'll briefly describe how I faced mine.

Most of us want to avoid pain as much as possible, but just like we would attend to a cut on our arm, we must also attend to the emotional wounds we suffer. I'm actually encouraged that we are becoming more willing to talk about emotional and mental problems like trauma and PTSD. We're finally coming out of that shaming tactic of telling people to "Just get over it!"

As I faced the many issues of my childhood, I was occasionally shamed by pastors for telling people I was going through a hard time. Most people who suffered what I experienced as a child don't even make it. They end up being alcoholics or drug addicts, and die without the Lord.

It took great courage for me to face my fears and ask for help. I'm glad God sent me the right people at the right time to help me overcome my brokenness. Unfortunately, there is a big misconception that, if a Christian suffers, he must be lacking faith, or is stuck in a sin. God uses times of suffering to make us aware of some issue that He wants to heal. The longer we run from it, the longer we will suffer.

This is a big problem for those who go to church seeking real help for real problems. Not only is God not bothered by our shortcomings, but that is the avenue He uses to teach, heal and grow our understanding of Him. He becomes real to us through our human sufferings. Our sufferings are only meant to last until we learn what lie we're believing that is causing us to suffer. Our pain is meant to lead us to the Father to find help and truth that corrects our beliefs.

This is a good time to clear something up. We ask, "If my sins are forgiven, then why does it seem like God is punishing me?" Our sins ARE forgiven when we give our heart to the Lord, but we still have false beliefs that prevent our souls from knowing the truth of God's love.

He allows us to be triggered in our false beliefs just enough to help us address the issue that lies buried in our heart. If the truth sets us free, then believing lies keeps us in bondage. Our spirits have been sealed unto salvation, but our thoughts and emotions and beliefs need to be corrected for our own benefit. He loves us enough to correct our harmful beliefs. He is not punishing us even though it may feel like it.

Some churches now offer grief ministry, AA classes, NA classes and divorce care to the community, but it can be hard to find compassion from Christians who have not been through our particular pain. Remember, the church is a place for broken people looking for their own answers, so we can't expect perfection from people, only from Jesus.

I was just talking to a man last week that said his family was asked to leave the church because his mom and dad got a divorce. What is the church here for, but to help people heal; not to reject them in their time of need. This has to stop. It grieves the very heart of God.

It's time to speak the truth about why God allows Christians to suffer. First of all, Christians are just like unbelievers in the fact that we too make unhealthy and unwise decisions with our lifestyles. What we eat and drink are an immediate source of suffering. There is so much sugar in our diet it's unbelievable!!

Our food has chemical compounds in it that are destroying our bodies at a rapid rate. Many people are often irritable merely because of the enormous amounts of sugar that they are consuming. This is a major cause of the cancers that attack our bodies, and we tend to ask God why He allowed us to get cancer. It's not His fault, but He loves to heal people from cancer.

We also suffer because we chase "get rich quick" schemes, make unwise investments, fail to tithe (I know, touchy subject) and buy luxuries on credit. We don't exercise patience or wisdom in our financial affairs because we want to keep up with our neighbors.

Remember, the 10th commandment says don't covet what your neighbor has. Work hard, save up your money and pay cash as much as possible on vehicles and furniture, etc. Houses are a better credit investment because at least they gain in value through the years.

We also suffer along with other humans because of political reasons, rules and regulations and our susceptibility to the ever-increasing amount of scams. If we will go back to our prayer closets and acknowledge God in every matter, then we can avoid making unwise decisions that cause our own suffering. This is one of the most practical and powerful passages in the Bible.

"Trust in the Lord with all your heart. Lean not on your own understanding, but in all your ways acknowledge Him, and He will direct your path." Proverbs 3:5-6

This is so simple in theory, but can be hard to practice, because we think we know what's best for us. Again, our human nature is selfish and unwise, but if we will just involve the Lord in our decisions, He will never lead us astray.

About a year ago I had my eye on a cool muscle car from the 1970s that was selling for $35k. I had the money, and I had almost no debt, but I asked the Lord if it was ok for me to buy it. He said, "Sure. You have the money, you can buy whatever you want, but are you sure you really want that particular car?" He spoke in such a kind manner.

As I thought about my ideal sports car, I determined that I really wanted either a Mustang or a Camaro, so I passed on that car. One or two weeks later I was looking through Craigslist and found a 2006 Mustang, blue with white racing stripes, 79k miles, for a 4th of the price of that other car! I bought it on the spot and now I get compliments everywhere I drive it.

If we will just invite God into our daily decisions, we will find out how kind and gracious He is to bless us with good things. Our Father loves us and wants us to enjoy our lives, but He wants to be included in our decisions so He can bless us with the desires of our heart.

Now for a more serious topic…suffering because of other people's sins. The book of James puts it like this…

"Consider it pure joy, my brothers, whenever you face trials of many kinds, because you know that the testing of your faith develops perseverance. Perseverance must finish its work so that you may be mature and complete, not lacking anything." James 1:2-4

Years ago I was complaining to the Lord about how certain extended family members seemed to reject my wife and I. We would eagerly ask about their lives and how they were doing, but rarely got the same kindness shown to us. The Lord told me very plainly, "Don't take it personally. You don't know why they act like that, maybe they are going through something that makes them closed off." I appreciated the advice.

We suffer needlessly when we expect people to treat us as well as we treat them. Our expectations of them, when not met, causes us to imagine all kinds of evil thoughts that torment us. It's better to take whatever they are willing to give and be grateful for it, than to expect what they are unwilling or unable to give. And here is another misconception that causes us to suffer.

We are not being wise when we say, "That person made me feel bad." Nobody can actually make us feel a certain way. Don't turn me off here, because I've suffered greatly from saying that, and I want you to understand. If someone's action triggered an emotional response, you already felt that way about yourself to begin with. Their action didn't make you feel that way, their action just REMINDED you that you already feel that way in your heart. Here's an example.

I was walking along a park trail today, and I passed several people coming my direction. Only one of those people acknowledged my presence at all. I was tempted to think that they were rejecting me as a person, but that feeling did not stick in my mind. I no longer assume someone is rejecting me because of the way I look or act.

I realize that most people are afraid to make eye contact with strangers anymore, and that has nothing at all to do with me. If feelings of rejection had overtaken me because of their actions, then they were just reminding me that I already felt rejection in my heart for some other reason.

In my heart at this time in my journey I had many triggers to hurtful emotions. The Lord helped me to see patterns of thoughts and emotions that made me feel bad about myself. As I experienced a feeling of fear, abandonment, etc the Lord would show me where that feeling originated from. For example, certain memories of my childhood would pop into my head at times, reminding me of bad feelings. When they did I would ask God, "What lie did I take on from this experience?"

One memory was of me as an 8-year-old looking out the window on a Friday night. My soon-to-be step dad promised to take me to the races that night, and he never showed up. I looked out the window for him to drive up every 5 minutes for 2-3 hours that night. He had forgotten about me, and later apologized in an unconvincing manner. This memory haunted me for years, causing me to take on rejection and abandonment feelings from men. I felt that daddys wouldn't ever care about me.

The Holy Spirit brought other memories to mind during this time of restoration. Sometimes I saw Jesus show up in those memories and reverse the lie that I had believed. Sometimes the Lord allowed me to enter a memory as my adult self and comfort my child self in that memory.

In this way, facing the memories that made me suffer was actually working to benefit me. This is how our sorrows and sufferings ultimately lead us to healing and strength. Listening to my feelings would make me ask questions about those memories. Then the Holy Spirit would expose the lie and reveal the truth of the matter. It's really that simple to heal our emotions. The biggest challenge is to listen to our heart.

Another recurring memory was of me in a daycare right after we moved to Lubbock. Two kids sitting at the table with me were being very mean to me as we colored in our coloring books. One kid snatched the crayon out of my hand, even though there were many others to choose from. I felt very unwelcome in that home.

The Lord told me, even though I felt rejection from those kids, He used it for good in the end. I have always had compassion for any newcomer in a group that I've been a part of. I will regularly go out of my way to welcome someone who is new to our group. The Lord told me that the daycare incident created compassion for newcomers into my heart, and that is a very good thing. As we confront our own sufferings and learn from them, it creates compassion for others who also suffer.

I'll close this subject of suffering with a few passages of scripture.

"Dear friends don't be surprised at the painful trial you are suffering, as though something strange were happening to you. But rejoice that you participate in the sufferings of Christ, so that you may be overjoyed when His glory is revealed. I Peter 4:12-13

"Humble yourselves, therefore, under God's mighty hand, that he may lift you up in due time. Cast all your anxiety on him because he cares for you."

"And the God of all grace, who called you to his eternal glory in Christ, after you have suffered a little while, will himself restore you and make you strong, firm and steadfast." I Peter 5: 6-7 and 10

CHAPTER 12

MARRIED YEARS

In January of 1985 I decided to return to Lubbock and finish my degree at Texas Tech. It was hard saying goodbye to the wonderful people of Palestine that had been so instrumental in my healing journey. So much had changed in me that year, most importantly, my heart opened back up to the Lord. As I returned home to Lubbock, the surroundings were the same, but I was different. Once again, I was excited about my future, and what it might bring.

It most definitely takes courage to face our fears and admit we have broken places in our heart, but it felt so much better to feel the closeness of God instead of emotional torment. I prayed and read my Bible a lot during this time. I got my old job at the RV dealership back and enrolled in school again.

At this time in my life I would regularly go running after supper to a nearby park, then I would pray as I walked home. I had some great conversations with the Lord during these times. I learned to listen for the Holy Spirit to speak to me during these times.

One night as I was asking the Lord what he wanted to do with my life, he gave me an earful. He gave me a prophetic word about 3 things that I would accomplish in my life. He said in my lifetime I would run my own business, I would write a book, and that He would use me to minister His love and acceptance to people who have been hurt in relationships. I thought that was very interesting, but I just kept those things to myself for the time being.

I left the job at the RV dealership and started a landscaping business in 1985 to help pay for college. When I graduated from Texas Tech in December of 1992, I was already making four times what I would have made using my college degree, so guess what I chose to do? I've just retired from my landscaping business after 37 wonderful and very profitable years!

I continued to gain more and more trust in the Lord as I finished up my college degree and started up my landscaping business at the same time. It took me 11 years to get my degree since I was paying my own way, starting and stopping a few times in between semesters. I'm grateful to the Lord for helping me become the first college graduate in my family for as far back as anyone can remember. That was a huge accomplishment for me, and it gave me confidence in myself and in the goodness of God.

In fact, while I was in graduate school, I found out from one of my dad's cousins that I had a great grandmother who was a full-blooded Choctaw Indian. My sisters and I were the last generation to qualify for government benefits, including free college and a free house, if we wanted to move to Oklahoma. I could have had all of my college paid for by the government! Wish I had known that ten years earlier, but God was faithful to help me pay my own college expenses.

I met a young lady from church while in college and we married the year after I graduated. Since I had no example of what a good marriage should look like, I just took on the mission of working hard and meeting all of my wife's needs. I had to prove to her that I was a good man and a good husband. Since I had been a people pleaser all my life I thought I was up to the challenge.

All I knew was that I wanted a safe, loving, happy marriage with no yelling or fighting. I couldn't wait to become a father, and after 5 years of marriage, we found out we were expecting our first child. I actually assisted in the birth of our firstborn… our son Jacob.

Being the only boy in my family with two sisters, two step sisters and two half sisters, I was elated to have a son! Two years later another son, Aaron joined our family; and two years after him, our only daughter Macy was born.

Just as expected, I loved being a daddy to my 3 kids! It was the thrill of my life, and I actually relished the responsibility of taking care of my family. Before having kids I would play golf, city league basketball, football, softball and volleyball, but many of those things got phased out with each new child. I didn't care though. This was what I was made to do, and it was very fulfilling to be their daddy.

One of the blessings of being a husband and a father was gaining new understanding about God. The love I had for my children helped me understand God's grace towards me. I began to think about God as being my Father. This passage of scripture reveals how God wants us to think of Him.

"How gladly would I treat you like sons and give you a desirable land, the most beautiful inheritance of any nation. I thought you would call me 'Father' and not turn away from following me." Jeremiah 3:19

Changing diapers and picking up their messes didn't change my love for them in any way. These kids were mine, and I had nothing but love for them. In the same manner, I understood how God could love me even through all of my messes. My understanding of God as a Father helped restore my heart in many ways.

Unfortunately, the more kids we had, the more stressful life became. I was working 12 hour days at times when the kids were young, and my wife was working 4 to 5 days a week as a nurse. My wife and I started drifting apart as the kids' needs overruled our needs. We let our kids' demands take priority over our relationship, which was a big mistake. We were both middle children, both having the tendency to not voice our own needs, and the stress of it all started driving us apart.

What added to my wife's stress was my desire to be involved in ministry. I had been involved in some type of ministry since I was 16, and it had been an important part of my life. My wife was not as interested in ministry, so that took away from our sense of unity. I would have loved for her to join me in spiritual passions, but instead it divided us.

When I turned 40 we agreed that I should take advantage of a real estate course that we saw on tv. So, in the winter times when my landscaping business was slow, I began to flip houses to grow our income. Both of us were college graduates, so we wanted our kids to be able to go to college as well, and that takes money!

I was successful at flipping a few houses at first, then I got stuck with a house that wouldn't sell. All at once I had two house payments and an extra $1,000 a month expense to come up with. I continued to tithe my income to the church, so the Lord provided faithfully for all our financial needs.

The Lord told me through desperate prayers that he had a different purpose for that house, and that I would need to rent that one out for a while. I would discover that purpose 17 years later. As a landlord I heard every lie known to man about why my renters couldn't pay their rent on time. I didn't like being a landlord, but I grew to be more assertive with people, which was good for me.

In 2011 we built my wife's dream house in the country on a one acre plot surrounded by cotton fields. We hired a contractor to frame it up and finish out the main floor, but I actually finished out the huge basement and built an additional bedroom in the attic. I also built a 1200 square foot barn with the assistance of one helper.

When it was all completed, I remember saying to myself, "Now maybe (my wife) will respect me." You see, the first time I met my wife's parents I saw how wealthy they were, and I was intimidated at first. I knew if I married her I would have to make a lot of money to impress her. Even though our estate grew to over a million, it seemed that it was never enough for her.

A man will literally wear himself out to meet the needs of the family he loves, asking only a "Thank you" in return. I was never demanding of my wife; I was too busy trying to please everyone else and be a good husband, father, provider and Christian. From childhood I had learned to not be a bother to people, and to deny my needs.

At this time I was an active deacon at the biggest church in Lubbock, had two jobs, helped to coach our kids sports teams, and helped run a concession stand on Friday night home football games to pay for Jacob's band expenses. I was very busy, but at least it was a good kind of busy. I experienced a lot of success, even though it didn't seem to impress my wife. She rarely celebrated my successes.

One day, when I had just finished a big project, instead of celebrating my accomplishment, she started praising two other men for their accomplishments. That ain't right. As we were moving to our dream home, I noticed all but one of my many sports trophies were gone. She had thrown them away!

We had both experienced a measure of child abuse, but it affected us in different ways. We were both codependent, but on opposite ends of the spectrum. One of us was the giver and the other was the taker. The giver had no healthy boundaries, and the taker had rigid boundaries. That dynamic worked fine until I woke up to the fact I was being taken advantage of.

Having grown up with abuse, I just allowed myself to be abused by many people throughout my life. For 55 years of my life I had no concept of what a healthy boundary was, how to speak up for my needs, or even to allow myself to have needs. I'd been so disappointed with having my desires go unmet that I just suppressed them.

I have a good idea what caused the change of heart in her towards me. I published my first book, God Hasn't Forgotten You, in 2009 and began to give my testimony in churches and to youth groups. At the same time my wife experienced betrayal at work, lost her position of influence, and was demoted. She was devastated, and having to listen to my testimony at that time irritated her greatly.

I was soon asked by a long time friend to help pastor his small church in Lubbock, and I gladly accepted, but she was not having it. She didn't want to leave our position of influence at Lubbock's biggest church to humble ourselves and serve in one of the smallest. This was a dream for me, but a nightmare for her, unfortunately. She grew up in a family that never talked about their personal problems, so she was programmed to devalue people who were emotionally open, like me.

All during my adult life I said, "I'll never get a divorce. I'll never do that to my children." Remembering how hard it was on me to go through three divorces as a child, and always hearing in church that divorce is an unforgivable sin kept me in an unbalanced marriage for much longer than I should have stayed.

But at least I was present to raise my children during their most formative years. Sometimes things don't work out, and it's better to leave than to stay in a toxic relationship. There is so much more I could say, but for my children's sake I will refrain.

I would never tell someone to dissolve their marriage, but I do encourage civil confrontation and setting healthy boundaries to see how they respond. Don't just put up with abuse. The one thing that God hates more than divorce is for his children to suffer ongoing abuse. 2 Timothy 3:1-5 says,

"But mark this: There will be terrible times in the last days. People will be lovers of themselves, lovers of money, boastful, proud, abusive, disobedient, ungrateful, unholy, without love, unforgiving, slanderous, without self-control, brutal, not lovers of the good, treacherous, rash, conceited, lovers of pleasure than lovers of God— having a form of godliness but denying its power. Have nothing to do with them."

That's a pretty rough passage of scripture, but it is very serious to the Lord. He is a protector of his loved ones. He would rather you escape a bad relationship than to have your soul destroyed by envious people, even if they are in your own family.

My children didn't see the abuses that I endured behind closed doors, so they lost respect for me, believing the lies that I was being selfish and uncaring. My kids stopped responding to my calls, texts, letters and gifts, like thousands of other men and women who dare to leave an abusive relationship.

There is no reason to destroy an ex-spouse after a divorce. Just go your own way and find peace, but don't destroy innocent lives, and alienate children from loving parents. I grieved the loss of relationship with my children for 3 solid years, crying an ocean of tears over them. The Lord was very close to me in those days, confirming His word that

"He is close to the brokenhearted, and he sustains those who are crushed in spirit.

Psalm 34:18

Those years of grieving and soul-searching were lonely and gut-wrenching. I faced accusations from people I loved, from the devil, and from myself. People I thought were my friends turned away from me. You find out who your friends are in times like that. I was basically isolated from everything I'd ever known except my job and my God. Instead of being a leader in church, I sat by myself in church, being avoided by most people.

I made light of my situation by saying the devil thought my name was Job, instead of Cobe, the name I was called by my closest friends. I certainly identified with Job, since I had lost so much in such a short time: my marriage, my children, my health, my church, my friends, and dozens of in-laws who I loved.

The Lord did send me a great friend who was in a similar situation as me. Greg and I visited several churches in town to see which one met the needs of single, older men. Greg even worked part time with me during those days, and it was a God-ordained friendship. We talked about a lot of issues and prayed for each other's healing from childhood traumas and failed marriages. I will always be grateful for Greg's friendship.

Through this isolation, I learned what it means when God is referred to as "Holy." I never had a grasp of what that meant, except the assumption that God was just better than us humans. I found out what makes God holy is the fact that He is different in every way from our other relationships. He never lies, never abuses, never manipulates or controls us, is completely faithful, and He has no selfish agenda for us.

He is special, He is different, He can be trusted when other people forsake us. Holiness refers to Him being different than anyone else we will ever encounter. He is family when our family disowns us. He accepts us when others reject us. There is no one like Him, anywhere!

And we are SO LUCKY that he chose to be good and honorable and selfless and kind. He could have been a tyrant if he wanted to be, but He chooses to humble Himself, to reach down from on high and lift us up from the pits we find ourselves in. I've never been treated by anyone as good and gentle and kind as He has treated me. He comes running when we call Him, and is always there when we need Him.

It took losing everything important to me to find out that I have all I really need. God took me from hating my isolation, to relishing it because of the peace his presence brought me. When my family forsook me, He validated me and redeemed me and adopted me. He is like none other. He is HOLY!

CHAPTER 13

DARK NIGHT OF THE SOUL

A movie came out in the early 1970s called The Godfather, about a man from Cicily that immigrated to the USA. As a boy, Vito Corleone learned to survive on the streets of New York City at the turn of the 20th century. He eventually started a mafia crime network that included his sons. At the end of the movie the family needed to "settle all family business" against people who had betrayed them. Several people were murdered, in order for the Corleone family to regain respect and power.

I've been intrigued by the Godfather trilogy for years, and I think I know why. I believe I enjoyed the power, strength and intimidation that the Corleones displayed. I longed to feel their power and strength. I'll admit, at times in my life I daydreamed about killing the people who hurt me deeply, but I knew that was not the way to get resolution to my pain. At this point in my journey, the Lord was telling me it was time to "settle all family business" but in His way. No, I never killed anyone…just in case you were wondering.

God's way of settling my business was to face the issues that had never been dealt with in all my years, things I was either unaware of, or too scared to deal with. I had to address the significant relationship problems buried under layers of shame and rejection.

Having lost the life that I had always wanted, I had nothing left to lose. I had no more fears to face; my greatest fear had already come upon me, and it hadn't destroyed me like I thought it would. But for my own peace of mind I had to make sense of it all, and fix what I could. I had to make peace with my past, and make my peace with God.

Even through the intense grief, the soul searching and the "dark night of the soul," I had a suspicion that this was all a part of God's plan for me. Through my own losses, a deep compassion for divorced and single adults arose in my heart. I remembered God's prophecy that I would one day minister to hurting people. I even had to call up some friends who had gone through a divorce and apologize for the things I said to them in the past. I always thought they just didn't try hard enough. I was naive to think that every marriage can or should be saved.

I had no idea that a lot of relationships are transactional and manipulative. We think by default that other people are just like us. Kind people think others are kindhearted, while selfish people think others are as selfish as they are. It's the same way with how people imagine God to be..

This passage says a lot about our perspective on what we think God is like.

"To the faithful you show yourself faithful, to the blameless you show yourself blameless, to the pure you show yourself pure, but to the crooked you show yourself shrewd." Psalm 18:26

This gives great insight into the heart of man, and how people routinely project their own beliefs onto others. When I remembered feelings of rejection from the past, I assumed others would reject me as well. Jesus summed up all of the commandments in the Bible into the two greatest commands. "Love the Lord God with all your heart, mind, soul and strength, and love your neighbor as you love yourself."

In my opinion, we automatically love others the same way we love ourselves. Those that don't love themselves are not capable of loving anyone else, but those who do love themselves are able to love others as well. And the only way we can love ourselves is to first experience God's love. The more we know His love, the more we are able to love ourselves and others. To know God is to know ourselves, because we came from Him. The very idea of you came from His heart.

When I was codependent, I loved people in a codependent way, by rescuing them from their own pain. Now I know the value in letting others take responsibility for themselves, and suffer the consequences of their own behavior. We must let people take responsibility for themselves, or they will never grow up.

For most of my life I forgave a lot of recurring abuses that I should have stood up to, but I thought it was my duty as a Christian to put up with abusive people. Now I know that is not God's way. He called out the Pharisees for their false piety and pride, and he will not let abusive people get away with it forever.

In a divorce recovery class, we were introduced to several great books on healthy relationships, my favorite being Boundaries, by Townsend and Cloud. I had never even heard of the concept of boundaries until I read that book, and it was life-changing for me!

Through that book I learned of my codependent tendencies and my lack of healthy boundaries. I learned so much about myself through reading that book, as well as Codependent No More by Melody Beattie. I'm so grateful for the kindness of these strangers to teach me a better way to relate to people.

That information should be taught in every High School in the world in my opinion. Why is this information so hidden from the general public? Possibly because the subjects of mental and emotional health have been stipulated as shameful through the generations.

We don't talk about these matters in public, and only those who have experienced abuse seek out this type of information and help. I'm glad that we as a society are beginning to address these taboo subjects more and more.

Many churches I've been to seem to be ill-equipped or unwilling to address these issues because they think good Christians shouldn't have those issues. Churches also stay away from adult singles' ministry for the same reason. Having been involved in Freedom Ministry classes for years as a student and as a facilitator, I've seen a lot of good and some not so good come out of it.

I hope to shed light on how the Holy Spirit sees mental and emotional wounds. The Holy Spirit is gentle, kind and patient with people, but I've seen some ministers treat hurting people harshly, hurting them even more, and it broke my heart for them.

We must stop shaming people for having emotional wounds. Maybe that's why the Lord wanted me to write this book, to show people how He has patiently and gently restored me to emotional health. Like I said earlier, those wounds need to be treated and addressed just like a cut on the arm. If we ignore the wound, it will only get infected and cause more damage.

As I wrote in chapter 3, we've been so conditioned by shame, we are afraid to admit our emotional struggles. Having grown up in Texas, I've seen the way good ol' boys treat their sons when they show vulnerability. Football coaches are notorious for using shame to motivate their players to do better. Calling someone a "sissy" can motivate a player to try harder, but I've seen that encouragement is much more effective when I've coached or taught something.

I'm so glad that God himself doesn't use shame on us; in fact, He wants to remove the curse of shame from us. Through walking out the process of forgiving my dads, I saw the great necessity of talking it all out. Most of us men just bottle up our feelings until one day our wounds are triggered, and we explode on somebody! I've been there and done that, even in front of my kids, which I greatly regret.

I suggest either finding a therapist, a trusted pastor, a trusted friend or most importantly, just go straight to the Lord. At first you may need to talk to a human, hopefully one who has gone through what you're going through. I don't recommend telling your relationship woes to someone who's been married for 50 years. They will not understand or be as compassionate as someone who has been through it themselves. This scripture explains the reason perfectly.

"(God is) *the Father of compassion and the God of all comfort, who comforts us in all our troubles, so that we can comfort those in any trouble with the comfort that we have received from God.*" 2 Corinthians 1:3-4

What I found out in my journey, is that emotions just need to be felt in order to pass. We are allowed to feel what we feel, even if it is based on a lie. Once we allow ourselves to feel our emotion, to let it say what it needs to say, we will no longer be held captive by those feelings. It's just about that simple. And if that feeling was based on a lie, we will eventually realize it was a lie.

After our divorce, I was left with a lot of questions to answer. Was I a good husband? Was I a good daddy to my kids? Was I wrong to pursue ministry opportunities? Why could I not find a healthy relationship in my life? These were gut wrenching questions that I had to be really honest about.

If you want to get God's attention… pray an honest, heartfelt prayer. Ask Him if there is anything you need to repent of, and He will speak clearly to you. I know He must get tired when we pray religious prayers that we think He will be impressed by, like the Pharisees used to pray. I know in my experience, when I pray an honest, humble sincere prayer, He shows up in a big way.

Psalm 139:23-24 says,

"*Search me , O God, and know my heart; test me and know my anxious thoughts. See if there is any offensive way in me, and lead me in the way everlasting.*"

I hated and feared being alone for the first few years after the divorce. I was left to deal with myself, my trauma and the devastating losses I had incurred. Even though I felt alone, the Lord was very close to me. He carried me through those times when I was overcome with sadness.

I read the book of Job to see if I could find any answers there. Then I read the story of Joseph in Genesis for any insights. I could relate to the losses and betrayal those men experienced, but I still wondered why God allowed such devastation to touch those Godly men. Job was the most righteous man in the eastern world back then. He feared God and shunned evil, so why did God allow such loss?

Job said the thing he feared most had come upon him. God himself said that Job was righteous in his consciousness towards the law of God, but there was something that needed to be corrected. As I read that statement it dawned on me that I had come face to face with what I feared the most...losing my family. They say those who love much, fear much. When you love people, your greatest fear is losing them.

I feared losing my marriage because I wanted to be married so much. I feared not being a good enough daddy because of my experiences as a child. Going through 3 divorces as a child made me afraid of being like my 3 dads. Those were subconscious fears that kept me from being the best husband and father I could have been.

I had to come to terms with the fact that I was not a perfect father, but I know no other human father ever loved his kids more than me. I was kind, gentle and supportive towards them. I was a great provider, and a great example of a Godly man, but not good at holding them accountable. I had to change my codependent ways.

I asked the Lord several times if He thought I was a good father to my kids, but He was reluctant to tell me. He knew that was something I had to answer for myself. I looked back over my years as a father and took inventory. I determined that I had never maliciously hurt my kids, and had been the best father I could have been.

I was invited to a men's group one night, and the message was about being a Godly father to our kids. I was not happy at first, thinking it would bring up bad memories, but it turned out to be a big blessing. They gave a long checklist of what a child needs from a father. Not only did I honestly check off every item, but I could double check many of those things. God was showing me that I really was a good father to my kids.

I still had irritating thoughts of how I failed as a father until one day, while driving to Dallas, I addressed the issue in prayer. I asked the Lord to redeem my relationship with my kids. Like Jesus blessed the loaves and the fishes to feed the multitudes, I asked the Lord to take my body of work as their father, and mix it with His grace to be enough for my kids. I prayed that my efforts would be good enough, and that God would make up the difference. I felt a release in my spirit, and the torment ended for good.

In the same way, I graded myself as a husband and determined that nobody had ever loved her the way I loved, supported and encouraged her. I was always there for her and eagerly tried to meet her needs. The Lord had me answer those questions on my own, because I had to learn to validate my own worth. God doesn't do everything for us. He wants to empower us with his truth to resolve our inner conflicts. He holds us responsible to fight for ourselves first, then He supports us in it.

I also discovered my codependent tendencies had led me to broken people all my life. There were some great, healthy women I could have married, but I was subconsciously drawn to the emotionally unavailable ones. My broken relationship with my dad set me up to chase and try to fix other broken, emotionally unavailable people.

This is why we go from bad relationship to bad relationship, until we resolve the fears and lies we've believed about ourselves. I don't completely understand how it works, but I know the process is to forgive, release the painful emotions and change the belief that we don't deserve happiness, in order to begin to attract healthy people to us. And we have to be honest about our own failures. We are all in need of change.

I began to settle my family business by honestly addressing my sins, releasing my emotional pain to God and forgiving everyone of their offenses, including my own. It was like cleaning out the cobwebs in my heart, courageously opening doors that had been locked for decades and facing the monsters hiding there. The funny thing is, those monsters were not really monsters at all, and they left as soon as I addressed them with the knowledge of the truth.

"Submit yourselves then to God. Resist the devil and he will flee from you. Come near to God and he will come near to you." James 4:7-8

Instead of murdering my enemies, I set them free from my judgments. I realized that we are all imperfect humans, and we all need God's forgiveness. This is serious business in God's eyes.

"For if you forgive men when they sin against you, your heavenly Father will also forgive you. But if you do not forgive men their sins, your Father will not forgive your sins."

Matthew 6:14-15

Well it just got real in a hurry! Remember, our pride has to be the first thing to go. We can't pretend we are better than anyone else. The smallest sin carries the same penalty as the biggest sin. We all sin, not one of us is innocent. Think of all the stuff we've done that we're ashamed of. If we want to be forgiven, we have to forgive. Even if you don't feel like it, speak it out loud and begin to heal. Set yourself free!

CHAPTER 14

RETURN TO INNOCENCE

Most of us are so busy distracting ourselves with external stimuli that we have no idea who we are inside. We are afraid to be alone with our thoughts, we rarely take inventory of how we are doing, and we're afraid of what we might find. Physical injuries are painful at first, but they subside as our body begins to adjust and heal. But emotional wounds scare us, and we are not taught how to deal with those injuries.

The Lord has graciously shown me how to address those wounds so that the trauma could be released out of my body, soul and spirit, so I could finally comprehend His love for me. I never wanted to know about the abuses that we inflict on each other, or how evil people manipulate and control us. I never wanted to spend 4 years of my life studying narcissism, just so I could have some closure to a 25 year marriage. I would rather have stayed naive, believing that people are basically good and want the best for us.

God had to show me the realities of human nature and of His true nature, so that I didn't end up in the alley somewhere as another statistic, or end up in prison. He revealed these things to me because of the covenant of love he made with me as a 10-year-old. I've discovered He is way more serious about us than we are about Him. I recently apologized to the Father for our lack of ability as humans to love Him the way He loves us. We can never match His goodness to us; all we can do is say a sincere "Thank you."

After I moved back to Lubbock from my time in Palestine, I started working at the RV dealership again while going to Texas Tech. One morning I prayed an unusual prayer. I asked the Lord to please show me His love that day. It felt like a strange and selfish prayer at the time; not like one of my usual prayers. I've come to understand that the Holy Spirit will impress upon me to pray a special prayer at times, when He wants to do something special for me.

After praying that morning, I went off to work as usual. Just before lunch I was working in one of our bigger motorhomes, one with several large windows throughout it. Suddenly, a sparrow flew into the RV, crashing into a window across from the entry door. Boom! The sound startled me, so I turned to see the bird shaking his head from the impact. We've all seen birds fly into windows.

When the little guy saw me he flew to the other side of the RV into another window! I was filled with compassion for the little guy and tried to move towards him. He flew away from me 3 or 4 more times, hitting a different window each time. He eventually ended up in the bedroom in the back to get away from me.

I thought, "Oh no! I need to help this guy find the door, so he stops hurting himself." As I walked into the bedroom, he was sitting on a window ledge, in pain and exhausted from the ordeal. I gently approached him, expecting him to fly away once more, but he just stood still, allowing me to pick him up ever so gently with both hands! As I walked him to the open door, I told him how sorry I was that he got hurt and that I wasn't going to hurt him. We made it to the doorway and I set him free from the "trap" he had gotten himself in.

He seemed to be pleasantly surprised at my kindness, flying away peacefully and slowly, even turning back in flight to catch another glimpse of me. It was as if he was surprised to find gentleness and kindness in someone his instincts told him was a predator. I had forgotten the special prayer that I prayed hours earlier, but after work I revisited the incident.

That night the Lord told me that incident was the answer to my morning prayer. He explained that the compassion I had for the bird is the same compassion He has for me. Just as the bird was scared of me, I'd been scared of God for much of my life, fearing He would be as mean as my coach or my alcoholic father. He was showing me a microcosm of my life in that 30 second event.

Like that bird, we find ourselves caught in a scary and painful existence, but our fear of God keeps us running away from Him out of our default sense of shame. Instead, we chase after any shiny object, any perceived window of opportunity, that might be a way out of our pain, only to just bang our heads on the disappointment of false hope.

Most people think that money, fame, recognition and human success are the ways out of our pain. We fight and compete against each other as if there is not enough love to go around. We don't feel good about ourselves because of our vulnerable, selfish disposition as humans, so we strive to at least be better than those around us.

We resent those who seem to be happy or have what we don't have, instead of rejoicing with them in their victories. God has enough blessings for all of us, but most of us don't seek Him enough to discover how kind and generous he actually is.

The Bible says "we have not because we ask not." Most Christians are working hard so God will bless us with a good life, but all we have to do is ask the Lord for what we need and want. We get mad at God when our hopes don't come to pass, but we haven't asked God for them. We just think God should give us a good life because we've earned it by being good.

That is an unhealthy religious mindset, and God doesn't operate that way. When Jesus encountered a blind man, He asked the man, "What do you need?" It was obvious to everyone there what the man needed, but Jesus made him ask in order to make a point to all of us. We don't earn points with God for being good. God wants a relationship with us where we involve Him in our lives. He does not want a business relationship with us. He wants a family relationship with us.

The Lord who created us, who gives breath to our mortal bodies, wants us to know that He has been grossly misunderstood and misrepresented. He is NOT the mean, tyrannical overlord he has been made out to be. He is truly the Father to the fatherless, the defender of widows and orphans and the One who deeply desires to restore our souls. He just wants to be with us during all the ups and downs of our life.

Like the bird, God just wants us to be still, come into His presence, and let Him reveal the truth about how much we are loved and forgiven and accepted, even in our imperfect human condition. When we look into our bathroom mirror we see a lot of imperfections, but God implores us to look into his mirror, the Word of God, so we can see ourselves through His eyes, and through the blood of Jesus. (James 1: 23-26)

He is the one who designed us, so He knows how to repair us, body, soul and spirit. For most of my life, I thought God needed me to work for Him, like my step dad wanted me to work for him. I asked many times, "Lord, what do you need me to do?" I had a performance mentality towards God, like nearly every Christian has, where we try to buy God's love.

Listening to church sermons for many years gave me the idea that God needed my help to save the world, but the Lord actually told me recently, "I don't need you to do anything for me." At first I thought that was the devil talking, but that has consistently been God's response to the hundreds of times I asked, "What do you need me to do for you?" Somewhere I picked up the idea that I needed to do something big for God.

One day while I was sitting on the front porch of our dream house in the country, I asked the Lord if I had accomplished all He wanted me to do in ministry. He surprised me by saying, "I don't require you to do anything big for me. You have no idea how many lives you have touched by just living your life in relationship with me. The people you meet sense my presence because of how you treat them, and that is all I need from you." I had put so much pressure on myself to minister to people because of my codependency and from listening to religious manipulation in church.

It is so important and so freeing to engage in honest conversations with God. One line from a Chris Tomlin song says, "How majestic are your whispers." That is so true! Those majestic whispers of God in the darkest times of my life, set me free from so much bondage, and like Isaiah 45:3 says, it was so I would KNOW Him.

"I will give you the treasures of darkness, riches stored in secret places, so that you may know that I am the Lord, the God of Israel, who calls you by name."

God wants you to know Him, and He is calling out your name, but we are too busy being distracted. In my 50 years with the Lord, it is my understanding that God just wants to set us free from our sorrows and sufferings so we can return to the innocence of our childhood. He wants to free our hearts from the unresolved conflicts and shame hidden there.

Many of us had our innocence taken from us by imperfect humans, but we can empty the pain out of our hearts by being present to listen to what our heart is telling us. We can trust God with the care and safety of our heart as we face the fears, the shame and our sins. He remembers that without Him, we are just dust, and so He provided a bridge to connect Him and us through the sacrifice of His only Son Jesus.

This is the message of this book and the message of THE BOOK, the Bible. King David was a man "after God's own heart" and had a very close relationship with God, even before the Holy Spirit was sent to the earth. This is how he described the nature of God…

"Praise the Lord O my soul, and forget not all his benefits— who forgives all your sins and heals all your diseases, who redeems your life from the pit and crowns you with love and compassion, who satisfies your desires with good things so that your youth is renewed like the eagle's. The Lord works righteousness and justice for all the oppressed.

The Lord is compassionate and gracious, slow to anger, abounding in love.

...he does not treat us as our sins deserve or repay us according to our iniquities.

As a father has compassion on his children, so the Lord has compassion on those who fear him; for he knows how we are formed, he remembers we are dust." Psalm 104: 2-6, 8, 10, 13-14

In the immediate aftermath of my divorce, and the separation from my children, I felt so LOST! My dream of having a great family was destroyed. My sense of trust in humans was destroyed. My belief that one reaps what he sows was crushed. Life did not make sense anymore! All of my years serving the Lord and loving people seemed like a complete waste of time and energy. I was suffering from cognitive dissonance, which scrambled my sense of right and wrong, good and evil, up and down, etc.

"Am I really a Christian? Have I been deceived all these years? Have I just made God up in my head? I lived my life according to the Bible, so why did I not get the promises? Why is life so unfair?" My confidence in myself and God was temporarily out of service. I was suffering from a type of PTSD.

The word of God says He is close to the brokenhearted and that soon became very obvious to me. At times the pain was so bad I wanted to kill myself, but God would not allow me to remain in that state of mind. He was telling me by His closeness and compassion, "I'm not going to let you fall. I'm going to bring you through this."

I began attending Church on the Rock in Lubbock at that time, especially enjoying the long worship times. Those long worship times allowed me to connect with the Lord through praise, and releasing my hurts to Him. The Lord was very close to me in those worship times.

One morning during worship the Lord showed me a vision in my mind that I will treasure forever. I was feeling so lost, so betrayed and confused at the time, so the Lord showed up in this manner. With my eyes closed, I saw in my mind a faint image of Jesus in the dark. He offered his hand to me, saying, "Take my hand and follow me."

He led me into a dark thicket, on a narrow path where I couldn't see one foot in front of me. I had no idea what lay ahead, or where Jesus was taking me, but the fact that I was holding on to Jesus gave me a feeling of peace.

That was a timely vision that encouraged and enlightened me. Just the reassurance that Jesus was leading me through my darkness, was enough to give me hope. It re-established in my heart that HE was in control of my life, not me. I was to follow Him and trust Him one step at a time. It reminded me of one of my favorite scriptures of all time.

"I will lead the blind by ways they have not known, along unfamiliar paths I will guide them; I will turn the darkness into light before them and make the rough places smooth. These are the things I will do; I will not forsake them." Isaiah 42:16

Jesus wanted me to return to the childlike innocence of trusting in Him. That vision spoke to my very spirit that I needed to step down off the throne of my life and allow Him to take over His rightful position as Lord and "tour guide" of my life. The word says in Matthew 18:3,

"I tell you the truth, unless you change and become like little children, you will never enter the kingdom of heaven."

I have always been a visual learner; words alone rarely changed me. I'm forever grateful how the Lord was speaking to me in visions. When we acknowledge God, he will speak to us in a thousand different ways, whatever it takes to reach us. The Lord has spoken to me in so many ways; through the Bible, through music, through the testimonies of other believers, and through prayer.

I encourage you to return to the innocence of reading, studying and trusting in the Bible. The first chapter of John declares that Jesus IS the Word of God, so when we read the Bible, we are being exposed to Jesus himself!

A few years ago I was invited to join a group of people interested in prophecy. The atmosphere of prayer and ministry was so soothing to my soul, and it was a great atmosphere to receive from the Lord. We would meet once a month for prayer, praise and discussion of prophetic topics. One day I was running late, and thought about skipping the meeting, but the Lord said, "Go ahead and go. I have something for you."

The praise time we experienced at the start of the meeting was heavily anointed, and I quickly got "in the Spirit." With eyes closed and heart open, the Lord dropped another vision in my mind. He took me back to when I was 3 years old, playing at the park with my sister and daddy. He showed me on the ground crying after my dad had cursed and kicked me after my injury. Then the Lord showed me something supernatural that has forever changed my life.

I saw Jesus enter the scene, pick me up off the ground and into His arms, and smile at me with pure love and joy! My 3-year-old self stopped crying immediately and smiled back at Jesus with a look of complete joy! In that moment, Jesus drove away life-long fear, rejection and shame, and replaced the orphan spirit I had lived under with the Spirit of Adoption.

Tears streamed down my face as my heart was finally being set free from the grip of shame, from the feeling that there was something unlovable about me. I felt in my spirit that God was setting me free from a life-long belief that there was something inherently wrong with me. I did deserve love, no matter how some humans had treated me.

As I forgave the people in my life that had hurt me so deeply, the painful memories faded away, allowing the good memories to return. I can look back to my childhood and to my marriage, and hold on to the wonderful memories that God has given me. Now I can clearly see that I really had a great life! I accomplished a lot in my life, and enjoyed great success. It's as if Jesus was restoring sight to my blindness.

I encourage you to let go of your pride, remembering that we are all flawed as humans, and forgive those who have let you down. Be the one who breaks the unhealthy patterns that have been passed down to you. Enter into a conversation with Jesus about the condition of your heart, and let's become part of the solution. Jesus came to break every curse, and break the shame cycles off our lives. Let's stop competing with, shaming and manipulating each other.

There is enough love and blessing for all of us in the kingdom of God. So, to answer the question, "Where is God when it hurts?" He is right there with you, hoping you will give Him permission to reach out and help you. God is the only one you'll ever meet that has no selfish agenda for you. He is absolutely FOR YOU and your success. Let's humbly accept that we are vulnerable and selfish and even dumb at times, and accept the help of the One who designed us in the first place.

I have worked hard to be a good Christian, a good husband, a good father; to be a lovable person who deserves respect. I thought it was up to me to prove my value to the world and to God. He has shown me that His grace is sufficient for me. We can relax, accept His love and forgiveness and enter into the rest that He has provided. We can return to the innocence of our childhood, trusting in Him to care for us like a good Father. Matt.11:28 -30 says,

"Come to me, all you who are weary and burdened, and I will give you rest. Take my yoke upon you and learn from me, for I am gentle and humble in heart, and you will find rest for your souls. For my yoke is easy and my burden is light."

ADDENDUM 1

WHEN LIFE IS UNFAIR

We've all said this statement many times out of frustration, "This is so unfair!" We think we deserve better treatment from people and from God. I'm not going to use the shame tactic of telling you to "Just try positive thinking" or "Just look at what you have that others don't." Some of the things people tell us when we are really upset are just not helpful. There are real issues that need real answers.

I'll be really honest with you; if you have not given your life to Jesus, and entered into a real relationship with Him, where you talk with Him on a regular basis, then you have not given him permission to be involved in your affairs. He's not obligated to help anyone who hasn't given Him permission to be his God.

God will not involve himself in the lives of casual observers. Only those who enter into a covenant relationship with God get to experience His blessings. We have no right to blame God for suffering the consequences of our own selfish decisions. God responds quickly to those who come to Him in humility and repentance. Don't expect God to answer your angry, accusatory or entitled prayers. He resists the proud, but gives grace to the humble.

A lot of people just want to know how to manipulate God so they can have the financial blessings that are promised in the Bible. All these prosperity gospel preachers on TV are leading so many people astray by making people thirsty for God's toys instead of God himself. I've engaged in this activity as a child. The main reason I wanted to play with a certain friend was because he had really cool toys!

Those preachers represent God as Santa Claus, or a Genie from the lamp where all you gotta do is rub him the right way, or say the magic words. God will not be manipulated by humans; He knows what's in the heart of man. He is not gullible and naive like we are. Galatians 6:7 says,

"Do not be deceived: God cannot be mocked. A man reaps what he sows."

So, unless you are a real child of God, you are not under His protection, and you are susceptible to every predator out there. I'm just being real with you here. But for those who ARE true believers, having been adopted by the Lord and are growing in the knowledge and understanding of His ways, you have certain rights and protections.

I have suffered what I felt were very unfair circumstances in my life, suffering great losses because of betrayals and lies spoken about me. I thought it was unfair that I didn't grow up in a happy family with a great daddy. But God did answer my prayers for a good father, just not one with skin on. He answered my prayer with the best father ever…Himself! God is the most generous, kind, honorable father there is.

So, many times we just haven't received the answer to our prayers yet; God isn't finished working things out yet. Right now, I'm praying for a Godly woman to spend my remaining years with, but I haven't found her yet. I am tempted to think God is being unfair because I was a good husband to my ex-wife, and I deserve a second chance.

God told me a few years back that the reason He hadn't sent someone yet was to give me time to heal from the divorce, and discover what kind of woman I really need. Many times God is not saying "no," He's just saying "Not yet." God IS being fair to us.

Now let's talk about the betrayals that God allows Christians to experience. How can a loving God allow his own children to be betrayed and suffer loss? That doesn't sound very loving or protective. I've never understood why God allowed Satan to destroy Job's life when Job was "blameless and upright, who feared God and shunned evil." If even righteous people suffer unfairly, then we are all susceptible to it.

What I discovered by studying Job's story was that, "What I feared most has come upon me." Remember that God wants us to face our fears and overcome them, even if we fear losing our family and our wealth.

As a father of 3, I feared losing my family more than any other thing. I had invested the best years of my life, the years of my physical strength and my emotional strength into my family. I wanted a family so much that I made them my idol by thinking they would meet the deepest needs of my heart. When I lost my family through divorce, my greatest fear came upon me.

But God, in all of His mercy and kindness, showed me that the true desire of my heart was to know Him intimately. My wife and kids could never fill the empty place in my heart that only God could fill. I had to lose everything important to me so that I could find what I truly wanted, a Daddy to love me. Jewish people call God "Abba," which means "Daddy."

I know there is some cliche' out there about 'losing what you can't keep to find what you can't lose,' but I don't want to cheapen the subject. In my landscaping business, whenever I lost a regular customer for some reason, God was always faithful to bless me with at least two more customers in its place. No joke; it happened a lot. So I learned to trust that my business losses were actually promotions in the long run.

My friend Hector recently lost his job, and I just happened to be working at his house the day he was let go. When he told me about it, God impressed in my spirit that this was going to be a promotion for him. I prayed the prayer of faith over him that day, and before his health care benefits ran out, God promoted him to a better paying job with a better supervisor, while keeping all his health benefits! God is faithful to protect and provide for those who trust in Him.

I'm not completely sure what Job had to learn from his sufferings, maybe that his righteousness was not what mattered most; that he must trust in the grace of God instead of his own "goodness." I know that's what I had to learn from my betrayal. I don't deserve God's blessings because of how good I am, but because of how good God is. He doesn't love us because we are good; He loves us because He is good!

When Job's sufferings ended, God restored double of all he had lost. I have experienced a double portion of some of the things I've lost because of betrayal. My kids are still estranged from me because of lies told by other family members, but God has promised restoration at some point. A good friend of mine, after hearing of my betrayal, received a word from God for me. It was a passage of scripture from Zephaniah 3:17-20 in which some parts have already come to pass.

"The Lord your God is with you, he is mighty to save. He will take great delight in you, he will quiet you with his love, he will rejoice over you with singing. At that time I will deal with all who oppressed you; I will rescue the lame and gather those who have been scattered. I will give them praise and honor in every land where they were put to shame. At that time I will gather you; at that time I will bring you home. I will give you honor and praise among all the peoples of the earth when I restore your fortunes before your very eyes."

Wow!! If you read the stories in the Old Testament, you will see that God loves to restore things and people. The 2nd chapter of Joel says that God will restore the years that the locusts have eaten, and He certainly has done that in my life. When we forgive others and make peace with our past, all of the sweet memories return to us. We can see that we really had a pretty great life after all.

There is nothing in our lives that He can't either restore or replace. We don't have to fear losing anything. If we lose something dear to us, He will replace it with something twice as good. Even when life is unfair, God will be more than fair to us.

Isaiah 61 tells us the reason Jesus came to earth.

To preach good news to the poor; To bind up the brokenhearted,

To set the captives free, To release prisoners from darkness,

To proclaim the year of God's favor, To proclaim that He will avenge us,

To comfort those who mourn, To provide for those who grieve,

To trade beauty for ashes, To trade gladness for mourning,

To give a garment of praise in exchange for our depression.

If God allows us to suffer unfair betrayal or unfair treatment, and we refuse to get bitter, refuse to allow hate and unforgiveness to take control of us—It gives God permission to bless us with a DOUBLE PORTION for all our trouble! I am seeing His double portion in parts of my life now, and I'm trusting Him to bless me with double blessings in my relationships as well.

The betrayal and losses I suffered crushed me like a grape in the winepress. It drove out my self-righteousness, allowed God to regain His place in my life as Lord, and gave me a heart of compassion for those who suffer. And since I've faced the greatest of my fears, I now have nothing left to be afraid of!

I know I can face anything in life because I know God will be with me no matter what life brings me. Since the Lord has met the greatest need of my heart with His own presence, anything else He may add is just gravy at this point. I've found safety and peace by letting God be God, and returning to my rightful place as his child. It took losing everything to gain what I had always wanted.

ADDENDUM 2

HOW TO LET GO

Every single one of us has a list in our head of the things we think we must have in order to be happy. Women probably have an actual list somewhere in their nightstand, lol! Men have a subconscious list that we are not even aware of. Our list grows whenever we see that our neighbor has something we don't have, or when we see a beer commercial on TV, or when we go to the mall. We look for happiness and fulfillment in external things.

These are the windows we crash into like that bird in the motorhome. I chased things on my invisible list too. The biggest items on my list were:

-Wife and kids, happy family

-become a pastor

-become a professional athlete

-have a house in the country

Sometimes gaining everything on our list makes us realize those things don't give the happiness we expected. Sometimes losing everything shows us what really matters, and who our friends really are. The bullies, the betrayals, the losses and the disappointments of my life led me to ask the deeper questions of life. When I suffered the greatest losses, I found that God was still there. I saw that He was the only one who didn't leave me.

The one I had given second place to most of my life made me a priority when I needed help the most. He left the 99 to rescue the 1. I was always looking for someone with skin on to make me feel loved. I didn't realize my heavenly Father was the one who could satisfy my soul.

In His love and wisdom, God doesn't allow us to be satisfied with the lusts of the flesh, the lusts of the eyes or the pride of life. He knows peace and contentment come from knowing Him. And we can't love ourselves until we know His perfect love. We were designed to desire a relationship with God. We have been so distracted away from our own soul's needs that we are just lost in the woods. We're looking for love in all the wrong places, as the song goes.

We suffer needlessly because of our list. "If I don't have this, that and the other, I'm not going to allow myself to be happy." That is how we sabotage our own happiness! I was devastated to lose the relationship with my children, but I eventually had to let go of my demands, and allow God to meet my needs in his way and his timing.

God allowed me to release all my hopes and desires into his care, trusting that He is in control of my life. He has always provided whatever I needed, so I can trust that He will continue to meet my needs. He also wants to give me the desires of my heart with things that He deems best; I have routinely been content to settle for less than best.

When we let go of our rigid demands for ourselves and of others, we set ourselves free from emotional torment. As Christians, we can place our trust in God's goodness, and rest in the understanding that He will provide what we need at the proper time.

We don't have to demand, push, manipulate or control anyone or anything to get our needs met. We don't have to beg people to love us, because our source of love comes from God himself. That is why God says, *"Seek first the kingdom of God and his righteousness, and all these things will be added to you." Matthew 6:33*

As I wrote in the first chapter of this book, we usually don't make the right decisions until we've made all the wrong ones first. We don't have to be perfect; we all have to learn how to walk. As one year-olds our parents celebrate every small step we take.

They don't shame us as we're learning to walk, they praise and encourage us. Likewise, the Lord is so proud of us when we try to walk in His ways. He knows we fall often, but He is cheering us on the whole time.

He is not ashamed of our failures or our bad decisions, as long as we are honestly trying to walk with Him. We suffer when we mess up, and it's okay. There is no more condemnation for those in Christ Jesus who walk by the Spirit, and not the flesh. We are safe in God's care. When we fall He will pick us up and stand us on our feet again.

The day I walked out of our dream house in the country, I was able to move into that rental house that God had that special purpose for. It was to provide a soft landing as I made a really big leap of faith. God knew at least 17 years earlier, when I purchased that house, that I would need to live there at that time. How did He know this was going to happen? The same way He knew one day I would have my own business and minister to hurting people. It was all a part of His plan for me.

I'm convinced that life on earth has already been planned out, especially for the elect of God. Many of the prophecies of the Bible have come to pass, because it was God's plan for them to happen. We don't have to be afraid of anything that might happen to us, because God uses everything we face for our good if we are His. (Romans 8:28).

Two years after my divorce I was living in the house that we lived in when our younger two kids were born. I kept it as a rental, and moved into it to remodel it and eventually sell it. My right hip was worn out from all the landscaping, running and sports I had done through the years. The house needed lots of work and I just couldn't do it because of my bad hip.

I prayed the most Godly prayer of my life one night. I gave every single aspect of my life (house, possessions, kids, my future, my health) over to the Lord to do with as He pleased. I submitted everything to His wisdom and Lordship. Three hours later my house was on fire! My neighbor's house had caught fire, which spread to our shared fence, then spread to my house. The brightness of the flames woke me up just in time for me to escape with my phone and the clothes on my back.

Both houses were total losses by insurance company standards, but most of my possessions were saved, only smoke damaged. I got an incredible insurance settlement, sold the smoky rubble to an investor, and one month later bought a beautiful newer home in a great neighborhood.

In that one "act of God," the Lord restored back to me every financial loss of my life! Every time somebody screwed me over with unpaid rent or unpaid landscaping work, God returned back to me! He was fulfilling His promise in Joel 2 to restore the years that the locusts had eaten. I know He will restore my relationships as well.

We never have to fear losing anything we have. God will restore the lost years in an instant if we choose to forgive people's sins against us. The safest place to be, the most peaceful place to be, is under the Lordship of Jesus Christ. I have seen His unbelievable kindness to me for 50 years now. I can honestly say I'm glad for all of the disappointments, failures, bullies and suffering, because it led me to call on the name of Jesus, and He came running to help me! What God doesn't restore or replace, He will grant you peace over the loss.

Don't let the sufferings of life scare you away from God. He shows up the brightest in our darkest times. He is not punishing us and He is not mad at us; He is merely saying, "Come home my child. Love waits for you."

God bless you all, my fellow humans.